Totally Secure

Finding Peace and Protection in the Arms of God

DON WILTON

Copyright © 2005 by Singita, LLC

All rights reserved.

Published by World Publishing, Inc., Nashville, TN 37214
www.worldpublishing.com

No part of this publication may be reproduced,
stored in a retrieval system, or transmitted in any form by any means,
electronic, mechanical, photocopy, recording, or otherwise,
without the prior written permission of the publisher,
except for brief quotations in critical reviews or articles.

All Scripture quotations, unless otherwise indicated,
are taken from the New King James Version®.
Copyright © 1982 by Thomas Nelson, Inc.
Used by permission. All rights reserved.

Scripture quotations marked (NIV) are taken from the
HOLY BIBLE, NEW INTERNATIONAL VERSION®. NIV®.
Copyright © 1973, 1978, 1984 by International Bible Society.
Used by permission of Zondervan. All rights reserved.

Printed in the United States of America

1 2 3 4 5 – 09 08 07 06 05

Dedications

My wife, Karyn Ann:
Who took my hand in hers and never let go!

———————————

My children, Rob, Greg and Shelley:
Who have held their Father's hand as his best friends
in all the world! And now Annabeth, too.

———————————

My parents:
Who held my hand, even when I wanted to let go!

———————————

My parents-in-law:
Who accepted my hand and adopted me as their son!

———————————

My brothers, Rod and Murray:
Who have held hands with me through
the journey of life!

———————————

My Lord and Savior, Jesus Christ:
Without whose Hand I would be Totally Insecure!

Introduction

I feel great confidence in commending Dr. Donald J. Wilton's ministry because I know that his preaching and teaching are based firmly on the Word of God. Don's expository preaching at the First Baptist Church of Spartanburg, South Carolina, and by means of The Encouraging Word broadcast ministry, has been a great personal blessing to me.

It is my prayer that this book, *Totally Secure*, will bless your own life, and be a book you will want to give to others also.

Billy Graham
Montreat, North Carolina
Spring, 2005

Table of Contents

Dedications iii

Introduction by Dr. Billy Graham v

Table of Contents vii

Acknowledgements ix

Foreword by Dr. Ed Young xiii

Chapter 1   What Is This All About? 1

Chapter 2   What Does All This Mean? 15

Chapter 3   Confused Feelings 27

Chapter 4   Making Contact 35

Chapter 5   Am I Sensitive to Sin? 53

Chapter 6   Am I Submissive to God's Commandments? 71

Chapter 7   Am I Saturated in God's Love? 85

Chapter 8   Am I Spirit Filled? 111

Chapter 9   Am I Scripturally Convinced? 129

Chapter 10   The Journey 139

Acknowledgements

I have been so blessed throughout my life. I can never get over the fact the Lord Jesus reached down from heaven and picked me up with His mighty Hand. I cannot believe I have the privilege of being loved by so many. I cannot believe the Lord Jesus would allow me to be one of His spokesmen, telling others that what the Lord Jesus has done for me, He will do for all who reach out and take Him by His already stretched-out Hand. I am so grateful to the Lord Jesus for holding *my* hand, for showing me that the journey is as important as the destination, and for never letting go!

I am grateful to the Lord Jesus for...

The Lucky Teagues and the countless numbers of men and women who allow me to call them my friends.

The countless numbers of churches, conventions, and organizations across the world who have allowed me to share the wonderful news of Jesus.

The Fry Hymels, Max Thornhills, Robert Simmonses, Jack Holts, and countless numbers of incredible men and women who prayed for me, loved my family and supported every opportunity to tell others we can be *Totally Secure*.

The beloved School of Providence and Prayer, The New Orleans Baptist Theological Seminary, for giving me roots in my spiritual walk.

Allowing me to be Joseph to my precious blood family and Barnabus to my spiritual family.

Putting people like Chuck Kelley and Jerry Pounds in the center of my heart.

My beloved congregation at First Baptist Church, in Spartanburg, South Carolina. They are truly my family. They celebrate Jesus Christ and Him crucified in season and out! They have provided the validation that God honors faith alone!

The Board of Directors of The Encouraging Word who exemplify devotion to our walk by faith.

My secretary, Sharon Brisken, for her tireless work and devotion.

The Knights of The Round Table: Steve Skinner, Britt Dillard, Lee Foster, Kent Holt, Eddie Robertson, Clint Smith, Sam Davis, Steve Wise, John Young, Scott Stancil, Sal Barone and Seth Buckley, for entering into an unbroken covenant of love and service in submission to our Lord and Savior, Jesus Christ.

Dr. Ed Young for his life and ministry and for taking time to write the foreword for this book.

Dr. Billy Graham for his love, friendship and encouragement.

Foreword

Ask 10 people on the street what it means to be a Christian and you may get 10 different answers. Ask ten Christians in the church if they know for certain they are saved and going to Heaven and you just may get ten different answers from them, too. Their responses most probably would include such comments as "I think I'm saved," or "I certainly hope so," or "No one can be 100% sure."

Certainly it would be misleading to suggest that Christians never doubt or wonder about their salvation. The truth is, most of us have had those questioning moments. They seem to occur most frequently when we have distanced ourselves from God by sinful thoughts and actions, or periods of spiritual drought. We just do not "feel" close to God and we begin to wonder, "Am I really His child? Am I really saved?"

Using personal stories from his own life, along with a biblical study of 1 John, my friend and fellow pastor Don Wilton sorts through the confusion many people have regarding their eternal security. He clarifies the truth that being secure in our salvation has nothing to do with our feelings or emotions. In fact, it has nothing to do with our sins. It has everything to do with the grace of the Father, the finished work of Jesus Christ, and the ongoing ministry of the Holy Spirit.

As you read through these pages you will hear the heartbeat of a man passionate about seeing people come to a personal relationship with the Savior and teaching them to be His disciples. Don Wilton is a Great Commission pastor, called of God to take the Gospel into all the world–and he does just that through the outreach of his great church, his broadcast ministry and his preaching appearances around the globe. I encourage you to read on and discover Don's passion and gift for communicating God's treasure of truth. I believe *Totally Secure* will answer any doubts you might have about your eternal destination while encouraging you to move forward in your faith with freedom and assurance. As a child of God you can indeed find peace and protection in His arms.

>Ed Young
>*Pastor, Second Baptist Church*
>*Houston, Texas*

CHAPTER ONE

What Is This All About?

"I have been a stranger in a strange land."
— Exodus 2:22b

For me, it began thousands of miles away from the United States. I was just a boy—adventurous, inquisitive, endlessly naughty, delightfully determined, but inwardly angry by a child's standard. Today's textbooks would have it all worked out and clearly defined. Yesterday's textbooks had nothing much to say.

Boys and trouble are like hogs and mud: they go together. But too much mud and too much hog can lead to a horrible mess! Boys will be boys, they say. But too much boys being too much boys can often lead to a horrible mess.

I was just that, I believe. All boy with everywhere to go—alone. So while my physical body grew and matured, my spiritual being didn't know which turn to take. The crisis of faith that was to come was inevitable. I knew, yet I did not know. I was supposed to be, but "supposed to be" never had a foundation. I heard, but I could not hear. I watched but could not see. Was I secure in my faith or was I "sort of secure?" The crisis of faith for me was to wrestle with the question, "Am I really saved?" I needed to know that I was eternally secure.

Upbringing had much to do with that crisis of faith but, as I would later come to understand, upbringing alone could not be blamed for it. Sure, God does not have a family plan for salvation. I know that now. Just because my father would be in heaven did not guarantee that I'll get there. But my tumultuous early days played a big part in my journey to become totally secure.

I was the product of wonderful parents who, though undeniably caring and loving, were woefully ignorant of the fires that burn deep inside a young boy's inner most being. Dad was the only child of older parents who considered the rigors of boarding school superior to those of having to raise their son with a personal parental touch.

Dad's marriage to the gorgeous daughter of a proud Scot and his athletic prowess failed to produce in him any true inner transformation. The lonely insecurities hammered away at the already fragile innermost being of this champion motorcycle racer.

Mother was in her own world of art, dance and desperation. Her religiosity was shallow and her inner cry teetered on the edge of marital destruction, not unlike the feeling of empty abandonment known to all who stand on the edge of a great chasm.

By God's grace, this man was to encounter the only means by which true transformation in the human heart can be accomplished. It happened when I was a boy of six or so. It was radical. My father went from not knowing at all to knowing once and for all. Heaven became his destination and telling others about the certainty of it became his determination.

Their new-found relationship with Christ turned my parents in a different direction, turning them into parents who were totally secure in their own grasp and understanding of this God of grace and mercy.

But the boy was still there, and he had his own highway to travel. He had to wage his own war. *He* had to become totally secure.

And so the boy tagged along from one school to another–five by the third grade, to be exact. Having to study the elementary principles of language and science in a foreign language was frequently accompanied by the bullying tactics of savage teachers who ran riot with their freedom to whip little boys into submission. They scoffed and scorned in the privacy of their classrooms, which were more like the prison cells of Nelson Mandela's Robben Island than the seats of learning and constructive engagement they were intended to be. In public, they drew heavily on their Dutch Reformed religion to justify their covenant of separateness and cultural superiority.

Our parents meandered on in abject silence and paid homage to the establishment for no real reason other than apathy. Perhaps fear played a part, for the overbearing teacher was arrogant and powerful and loud and vicious. Besides, God was on his side. It just was not the Christian thing to do to oppose God's established authority for government.

So, here I was with two major spiritual earthquakes ready to shake any foundation of my impending Christian faith. One was that we moved frequently, which left me like a tree ripped up from its roots one minute only to be replanted elsewhere the next. And every time the tree was uprooted, the roots of the re-plant shriveled and became progressively weaker.

The second was the silent killer of faith which went by the name of a so-called Christian government that justified evil by the twisting and contorting of the Word of God, coupled with a firm belief that children should be seen but not heard.

In those days, though, I was getting ready to make my decision for Christ.

I also had two brothers. The older is changed today, for sure, but then...then he was selfish, arrogant and mean to the core. The younger seemed ... well, too young to me then. He is precious to me today. Three boys. One roof. All totally at peace today, all transformed forever, all the closest friends. All serving their God, all totally secure!

At the tender age of nine I was "invited" to enter the joy of "like father like son." That is to say, Dad sent me to boarding school. After all, it was paid for by some benefactor. Certainly it was a better option than the daily misery of the neighborhood school and environment I found myself in. On one occasion I was beaten up by a group of boys on the way home from school for no apparent reason. I watched open police brutality spurred on by the racist apartheid laws of the country in which I lived. I have a vivid recollection of our African maid wailing and screaming as the police whipped her husband to shreds for the "crime" of having spent the night with her in *her* quarters behind our house. My parents protested to no avail. On another occasion, my big brother gave me a lesson I shall never forget. I dared to ride his bicycle up the driveway. Needless to say, boarding school provided me with an opportunity to get away from it all.

My school nestled in the beautiful rolling hills of Zululand. To the north the majestic peaks of Champagne Castle and Cathedral Peak rose like warlords surveying their dutiful subjects. The Drakensberg Mountain Range ran rings around Chief Leabeau Jonathon's tiny landlocked Kingdom of Basutoland and then gave way to the glittering barriers of the gold reef. Both soon fell away into the war-torn ravages of the violence between Robert Mugabe and Joshua Nkomo's Patriotic Front and Prime Minister Ian Smith's unilateral declaration of independence from Britain.

To the east was the small Kingdom of Swaziland with its capital at Mbabane and its harvests of trees and plains of cattle. To the west lay the long journey to the beautiful Cape with its mountains, rivers, gorges and beaches culminating in the spectacular fragrance of the Cape of Good Hope, spearheaded by the command of Table Mountain. To the south spread the Valley of a Thousand Hills—every inch of which screamed with the blood of Shaka and Dingane's fearless Zulu Impi warriors, whose battle techniques were accompanied by the rhythmic chants of wave upon wave of death-defying battle cries, as each man lunged forward with his short stabbing spear.

There I stood, all alone in the big and frightening world of boarding school. Following my timely beating by the headmaster in the *Chicken Run* dormitory on the first night away from home, I found myself once again subjected to the tyrannical behavior of the power mongers. Fight to the top was the only solution, so I began to fight my way to the top with some success. Those days and years were filled with a mixture of fear, adventure and untold solitude.

The day of my conversion to the Christian faith arrived with no undue pomp or ceremony. I was home during the holidays when my parents led me to accept Jesus into my life. A little vague, perhaps, but it happened. After all, I was in Christian boarding school. We said prayers before bed time, learned to quote The Lord's Prayer effortlessly and possibly in Latin–and, most importantly, stood to attention before every meal and said, "For what we are about to receive we are truly thankful." At the end of every meal the entire school stood and dutifully said in unison, "For what we have received we are truly thankful." And so we learned to lie even to God who must have known how awful the food really was at boarding school, especially when every evening meal was preceded by a tablespoon of molasses and sunflower oil!

What exactly had I done at such a tender age? I had given my heart to Jesus Christ. I followed the script. I had the right people to administer the proper procedure. I exercised "childlike faith" which believed that God would do what God said He would do to those who call on His name.

But it didn't take long before the early fires of conversion began to simmer down. The coals gradually became separated from the fire. The burn became heat, then fizzled into insipid warmth. The warmth stammered, coughed and spluttered. Was I truly saved from my sin or not? If I died where would I go? How could I know for sure?

Let's not misunderstand this boy's life at this point. He was never outrageously bad, never malnourished. He was never given anything but the very best expression of parental love–never without the tenderness of a mother's loving care and ceaseless prayer, never without the distant firmness of a father's desire to mold and share.

This boy's life was filled with adventure of the highest order: surfing and diving off Bat's cave or Nahoon Beach, fishing for blues off the rocks into a magnificent Indian Ocean, playing cricket and rugby and hockey. Countless dream vacations to caravan parks nestled in the hills of Plettenberg Bay in the Cape and Saint Michael's-on-Sea on the Natal South Coast led to hitchhiking to remote areas of Mozambique, Swaziland and even the Orange Free State, stealing unsuspecting chickens from isolated farm houses and cooking them on open fires with a stick thrust through their roughly plucked bellies to provide the prehistoric rotisserie, or floating down the raging torrents of a swollen Little Caledon with not a stitch of clothing on, while clinging desperately to a rolling log intermingled with the bloated carcasses of wide-eyed animals caught in the cross currents of the after-storm. Or getting stranded on a precipice of the Wild Coast, arrayed in nature's splendid naturalness, overlooking the shark-infested mouth of the Umgazana River, as the boy's grandfather, Captain Roderick Murdo MacDonald, turned his ship around on a dime and headed back out to sea.

Now, a point of order is necessary here. This is all about people like you and me. I have met many people like you and me who gave their lives to Christ at an early age and have always been totally secure in the decision they have made. My wife, Karyn, is one of those people.

But here's what happened to me. Having turned my life over to the Lord, I immediately began to see practical results. There I was in the mountains of Zululand at boarding school with a willing heart ready to serve the Lord.

Many a Saturday and many a Sunday afternoon found this young pupil on a horse in the hills surrounding the school. All I had in my possession was a small single record player that had to be wound up using a sidewinder attached to the instrument. In a backpack of sorts I carried a number of records that had been produced by the Africa Inland Mission in the Zulu language. They began with a song followed by a message on the love of Jesus Christ. I would set up my station surrounded by round Zulu huts with grass roofs and mud walls made mostly of cow dung. Most of these homes had only one door and usually housed an entire Zulu family. These huts were organized in small compounds for protection from wild animals, as well as to accommodate Zulu customs of chieftainship and marriage.

Normally I would simply set up my station, wind up the record player, and watch as curious Zulus would begin to gather around. At the appropriate time I would share the love of God with them and then hand out gospel tracts before moving on to the next station.

The fact that "a new broom sweeps clean" was certainly true in my case. Perhaps that is when the Lord called me into the gospel ministry. But gradually over time, this fervor began to erode and fade. And with it went any security I may have enjoyed.

What happened? Well, I eventually left boarding school and moved to my parents' new pastoral charge hundreds of miles away. The move was not good for me.

I went from "top dog" at boarding school to "nobody's dog" at a huge all boys' prestigious high school. The top of the ladder I had fought so hard and hurt so much to achieve was gone—I'd fallen to the bottom of the ladder with a bunch of highly over-rated young English gentlemen.

Once again began the whippings with "canes" across the buttocks to the point of blood. My faith was being threatened in a serious way during the most formative years of my life. The foundation of my belief was at stake. I knew exactly what I had done some years earlier when I accepted Christ, but something was wrong. My total security was in jeopardy again. It was being eaten away by people, circumstances, and a desperate search for significance on my part.

One of my teachers didn't help matters. As the major Christian representative on the faculty, he took great pains to mock me while attacking the fact that my parents were in the ministry. His comments were always made in public and were designed to break down and belittle as much as possible. His public Christian persona and the weak strands of my relationship with Jesus Christ caused another collision in my already emaciated spiritual framework.

I rebelled. I sought out bad company with such relish that I soon *became* bad company. The streets became my backyard, while my heart closed with every passing moment. An inner anger boiled like the deep down cauldron of a killer volcano waiting to erupt. The church became my life sentence, and worship was regarded as a wasted opportunity. Hours upon hours of utter nothingness occupied my time, eating away at every opportunity to grow.

By the 11th grade in high school, almost everything was being thrown out the window. I was angry at life, blamed every person I could, took it all out on my parents who continued to love me despite all of this, and sauntered around as though the world owed me big time. My whole life became one big secret. I deceived my friends, danced my way from one party to the next, and all but denounced God.

The greatest casualty was my faith in Jesus Christ. Every time I heard my own father talk about the love of God my soul would break into a sweat. Youth camps became opportunities to prove my manhood and cause my father much grief.

By God's grace alone I graduated from high school despite having flunked the 11th grade outright. The First Special Services Battalion beckoned me for active duty and I was trained as an officer in the Armored Division.

This was the saddest chapter in my spiritual life, and it was not just because of my time in the deserts of South West Africa, now known as Namibia. I was sinning against God at every opportunity with little care in my heart. Or so I thought.

Was He even in there? If I died, would I go to heaven? Surely not! But then, what about the decision at boarding school? What about my faithful parents. I just didn't know. At least I had the comfort of no one else in our squadron of Desert Rats knowing whether or not I knew! They didn't even know what a Christian was supposed to be. They never heard about it—not from me, for sure! The absolute last thing I would ever admit to being was one of them! And when we had a pass for the weekend the drowning of our fears and sorrows was far preferable to even the slightest religious discussion.

It changed on the day that my orders came from headquarters. We were camped at Rocky Point not far from the Angolan border crossing at the Kunene River mouth. Our Centurion, Mark IV tanks and our Eland Armored cars were gathered across the desert in circle formations for protection. The Colonel told me to take a night patrol and surprise attack one of our own units some 50 miles away in order to test their military preparedness.

In the ensuing chaos of friendly battle with gunfire sounding, grenades exploding, and the merciless capture of "the enemy," I was thrown from my armored car and narrowly escaped death. Had I been killed where would I have gone: to heaven or to hell? How could I know for sure? I certainly did not "feel" saved.

My long-awaited discharge finally arrived with another seven day nightmare ride on a packed out troop train back to "civvy-street." The boy was now a man, ready to rumble.

But God had another plan. The girl! There she was, as beautiful as the eye had ever beheld, as serene as the tranquil view on Table Mountain, as majestically pure as the virgin snow.

With an unapologetic grace, this handcrafted treasure of God's grace led the perplexed man from the inner haunts of his spiritual insecurity to the point of total security. She gently took him by the hand

and nudged him with undue grace, forgiveness and spiritual understanding from the altar of marriage to the altar of a bended knee in the presence of the only one who could provide total security.

With my wife beside me I prayed a prayer something like this:

Dear Heavenly Father:

I have to talk to you. My heart is heavy and I am so confused. Many years ago, as a boy, I made a decision to give my heart and life to you. I think I was sincere. In fact I remember wanting to serve you so badly. But since that time it's all become mixed up. Sure, I have had many happy and good times. But, Lord Jesus there is a fire burning in me.

This morning, as I sat in church, I felt a deep moving in my heart. I don't know whether or not I am a Christian. Sometimes I think I am. But often I don't. When I go to church and the preacher gets going, I break into a sweat of sorts. Then I leave church and get all swallowed up in the things I do and forget about it for a while. Then it all comes back again.

I can't go on like this. I must know. I want to be totally secure. I want to know that when I die I will go straight to heaven to be with you forever.

Right now I confess all my sin to you. I believe that you died for me on the cross. I believe that God raised you from the dead. Please, Lord, come into my heart and save me once and for all. I accept you into

my heart by faith and I trust you with my life.
I pray this in the name of the Lord Jesus Christ.
Amen

Here's what I believe happened to me. If I was not a Christian when I prayed that prayer with my wife at my side, Jesus came into my heart then and there. If I was saved when just a boy, but had drifted away from the Lord, I was brought back home like the Prodigal Son. And I was given the absolute assurance that I would go straight to heaven to be with the Lord Jesus forever when I died. From that moment on in my life I have never again doubted my salvation. Yes, I have sinned many times against the Lord as a Christian. But the One who saved me is faithful and just to forgive me and cleanse me from all my sin. I am totally secure.

You can be totally secure, too. Throughout the world I encounter people struggling with this issue—good people, churched people, unchurched people—people from every walk of life.

This is what *Totally Secure* is all about. This book will radically transform you. Read it. Learn it. Inwardly digest it! Hold to the truths of God's Word. Lay aside all other distractions. Listen to none other than the Lord Jesus Christ.

There is surely nothing more important than knowing that you are going to heaven.

We begin with the meaning of salvation.

CHAPTER TWO

What Does All This Mean?

"It all starts with God."
— Rick Warren

Consider this question: How do you know for certain that God has forgiven you of your sin? Is it possible to really know that you are going to heaven one day?

This greater question presents little room for argument and even less room for misunderstanding. The Word of God provides a clear directive when it comes to giving one's heart to the Lord Jesus Christ.

In short, there are basically four requirements for salvation. The first demands repentance. In Acts 3:19 we are instructed to "repent, then, and turn to God, so that your sins may be wiped out, that times of refreshing may come from the Lord." There can be no salvation without repentance.

Adam and Eve were created by God as two perfect human beings in the Garden of Eden, but they sinned against God by eating the forbidden fruit. As a result, God threw them out of the garden because of their sin. This is what happens. Our sin, which we are born with, separates us from God. The reason that God cannot fellowship with us is that He is holy.

Repentance, therefore, carries with it the mandate to recognize and acknowledge our sin which "separates us from God." Furthermore, it indicates our willingness to turn away from ourselves and turn toward God. Recognition of our sin and identification with Christ are the two indispensable components of repentance. On the one hand, the sinner submits in acknowledgment of sin, while on the other hand the Savior spreads His arms of compassion to receive the undivided attention of the sinner He seeks to save.

The second requirement for salvation demands confession of sin to the Lord Jesus Christ. Some have a real problem here, but the Scripture is clear. His tireless teaching of the 12 disciples involved reassurance and instruction, especially considering their disbelief and consternation when presented with His imminent departure from them.

In John 14 one can hear the fear expressed in Thomas' plea on behalf of the disciples, soon to be fatherless and leaderless. "Lord, we don't know where you are going, so how can we know the way?" Remember, the Messiah had just unloaded on his boys. They depended on Him. They were in awe of Him. They had walked with Him and watched Him. They loved Him.

Now they hear the dreaded announcement. He was going to leave to go to a place which they knew nothing about. Evidently the guarantee of their accommodation in this place had been secured already, and Jesus Himself was going to provide the transportation needed to get there. And, to make matters even more complicated, God lived there too!

To the Jewish mind this was almost too much to handle—period. The disciples had heard the Pharisees accuse Jesus of blasphemy at this point, but they had no problem about how Jesus regarded them. Vipers came to mind! Notwithstanding the world's opinion, these men believed every word He shared. They stood up and were counted.

So, it seems rather significant that the Lord Jesus lays it on the line at this point. His claim to be the only way is based on the fact that He is truth. And because He is truth, He is the only one who could guarantee that a person could be secure for an eternity in heaven. The only way any person can join Him in this place called heaven is to go through the Son. Herein lies the essence of confession. No other person has the authority of God the Father to hear, accept and waive confessed sin.

The writer to Hebrews puts the argument squarely in the realm of absolute truth. There is no other way! Alternative solutions to the problem of man's sin are non-existent. Compromise carries no weight. Neither does political correctness. This is not open to debate and carries no possibility of negotiation.

Think about this: Our God, who is incapable of telling a lie, tells us that our hope is anchored in the sacrifice of the Lord Jesus upon the cross. Hebrews 6:19-20 (NIV) confirms this hope. "We have this hope as an anchor for the soul, firm and secure. It (Jesus) enters the inner sanctuary behind the curtain, where Jesus, who went before us, has entered on our behalf."

Formerly, the Old Testament High Priest was the only man permitted behind the curtain and into the "Holy of Holies." This priest was the one to whom confessions were made because he was the only one permitted to have access to God.

But that all changed at the cross. Jesus now is the only one to whom confession of sin is made. So it seems clear that we can be sorry for all the wrong we have done and express that sorrow to anyone we meet, but until we confess it all to Jesus Christ we sorrow in vain!

The third requirement for salvation concerns our belief in the resurrection of the Lord Jesus Christ. The person who wants to be forgiven of sin and know for certain that he is going to heaven must have a deep and abiding conviction that Jesus came back to life after He was put to death on the cross. Writing to the church at Rome, Paul put it like this:

> That if you confess with your mouth, "Jesus is Lord," and believe in your heart that God raised Him from the dead, you will be saved. For it is with the heart that you believe and are justified, and it is with your mouth that you confess and are saved.
> — *Romans 10:9-10*

Eternal life and the resurrection are intertwined. They are inseparable.

Consider the Corinthian Christians. They were a group of brand new followers of Christ. They had little chance to know much at all about their new-found faith, and not a whole lot was available to read about the subject. The city of Corinth was rampant with idol worship, prostitution and every known crime against humanity. These new Christians were eager to please the Lord, but they were extremely prone to worldly infiltration and given to excesses in many expressions of their new- found faith in the Lord Jesus.

Their pastoral teacher, Paul, gets down to business with a serious letter of instruction. Their talk needed to be matched by their walk. The "walking" of their faith would be considered critical to the "knowledge" of their faith. This became a manifesto of applied theology.

But the *practical application* of faith makes little sense if not grounded in the *doctrines* of the faith. In the letter to the Corinthian Christians we read about behavior, the matter of lawsuits, how to respond to idol worship, immorality and sexual perversion, and the list goes on. Even the great love chapter—in addition to the avalanche of detail regarding spiritual gifts—serves as a drum-roll to the glorious truths of the resurrection of our Savior.

Chapter 15 stands as the focal point. This is what it is all about; here we see ultimate faith. This faith is rendered futile without the resurrection; the church has no foundation without the resurrection; Our preaching of the Gospel becomes a waste of time and energy without the resurrection. Death remains a dark and dismal mystery bound by oblivious nothingness compounded by the winds of speculation and suspicion without the resurrection. The need to witness and testify becomes senseless without the resurrection.

Without the resurrection, Christianity becomes nothing more than a mockery.

Without the resurrection, the imputed righteousness of God in Christ would not be available. Preachers would have nothing to say! The pursuit of righteousness in Christ Jesus would be relegated to a fanatical group of Jesus "freaks" who would do no more than follow after fine stories and fables.

No wonder we are called to believe that God raised Jesus from the dead. Listen to the Apostle Paul:

> But if it is preached that Christ has been raised from the dead, how can some of you say there is no resurrection of the dead? If there is no resurrection of

the dead, then not even Christ has been raised. And if Christ has not been raised, our preaching is useless and so is your faith. More than that, we are then found to be false witnesses about God, for we have testified about God that He raised Christ from the dead. But He did not raise Him if in fact the dead are not raised. For if the dead are not raised, then Christ has not been raised either. And if Christ has not been raised, your faith is futile; you are still in your sins. Then those who have fallen asleep in Christ are lost. If only for this life we have hope in Christ, we are to be pitied more than all men.

But Christ has indeed been raised from the dead, the first fruits of those who have fallen asleep. For since death came through a man, the resurrection comes of the dead comes also through a man. For as in Adam all die, so in Christ all will be made alive.
— *1 Corinthians 15:12-22 (NIV)*

How is it possible to contemplate giving your heart and life to the Lord Jesus without believing in your heart that God raised Him from the dead?

Let me give you an illustration. Every trip to Israel brings inspiration and an abiding sense of joy—at no time stronger than when standing at the base of Golgotha. The empty tomb stands as a vacant hole in the wall. The shackles of death lie speechless and bewildered. The embalming cloth that wrapped our precious Savior and Lord lie crumpled in a pitiful heap of desperation like a marooned ship without water.

Here we see the hope of our faith. The stone had been rolled away, and that huge boulder was accompanied by the countless little stones of our human predicaments and fears. Who are we, where did we come from, and where are we going?

There's the stone. Look at it, standing useless and abandoned. Observe the stone, lying there in a ridiculous posture to be stared at by masses of redeemed sinners whose stone of sin was lifted at Calvary. There it stands in stark contrast to the power it once wielded when that bunch of tough army guys slammed the door shut on the One who had come to set the world free. Look at the stone, once proud of its accomplishment in carrying out its destiny. This was its life's purpose, to carry out the will of a mob's demand for the blood of an innocent man! Now look at it! Powerless and pathetic, nothing more than a sideshow. In stark contrast to its glory days, it now stands as a testimony that the grave could not hold Him.

> "Where, O death is your victory? Where, O death is your sting?" The sting of death is sin, and the power of sin is the law. But thanks be to God! He gives us the victory through our Lord Jesus Christ.
> — *1 Corinthians 15:55-57 (NIV)*

Any more questions about this third mandate for salvation? Have you believed in your heart that God raised Jesus from the dead? There is no alternative. There is no other way. This is God's way!

The Scriptures demand a fourth requirement for salvation. Trust in the Lord Jesus Christ by faith. This is the part of our salvation for which we should be most grateful. Our gratitude is well-founded because faith takes the initiative out of our hands and places the emphasis where it should be on our Heavenly Father. Salvation, in fact, finds its root, reason and response in the heart of God. Nothing else actually matters.

Take a closer look. We understand, that "all have sinned and fall short of the glory of God" (Ro 3:23). Not one person is worthy of being saved. Sin is the great divide between God and man. Our "Adamic" nature carries the condemnation of a righteous and holy God. He cannot tolerate our sin, and the result is eternal death. Man had to do something to gain forgiveness and be reconciled to God, but he failed miserably.

The Old Testament offers some of the best examples of man's failed initiative, his own effort to justify himself in the eyes of a holy God were rendered null and void. The priest not only offered sacrifices for His own sins, but also for the sins of the people (He 5:3). The problem was that he could only deal with one person at a time. Therefore, the people had to make sacrifice for sin, over and over and over again.

The great reformer, Martin Luther, understood this best when his bold initiative precipitated the Protestant Reformation in 1517. Luther had an awakening of the soul. God revealed Himself through His Word.

The light came on when Luther realized the significance of what the Lord Jesus had done on the cross. Jesus was presented by God as a sacrifice "through faith in His blood" (Ro 3:25), and this is why God is a just God. The sacrifice of Jesus demonstrates God's justice, and it all comes together by means of faith. Faith does not require understanding; understanding follows faith. Faith means the acceptance of all that God tells us, whether we understand it or not. Otherwise, it is not faith. I like that because it frees me from any futile human effort to try and figure God out.

Think about it. Who is God? He is King of Kings and Lord of Lords. He is the Alpha and the Omega, the beginning and the end. He is the first and the last. He is the great "I Am." In the Hebrew language Jehovah's name cannot even be pronounced! Evidently there are some who still think that they can understand God to the extent that their "modern-day Pharisaism" adds the component of understanding to the requirements for salvation. Surely not! In his discourse to the Ephesian Christians, Paul settled this issue once and for all.

> For by grace you have been saved through faith, and that not of yourselves; it is the gift of God, not of works, lest anyone should boast.
> — *Ephesians 2:8-9*

The absence of faith renders man's quest for salvation obsolete. Any attempt on man's part to merit total security conjures up the idea that man can work for or earn his salvation. As soon as personal merit attempts to usurp the grace of God, pride rears its ugly head.

Works relegate man to a bloody war. One battle follows another as religious denominations try to outdo each other in legalism and rules. Respective members fall in line to follow the rulings and opinions of their spiritual leaders as they hustle and bustle for a special seat at the right hand of God. Such futile endeavors become reduced to ridiculous proportions. Examples can readily be found in the giving of money, acts of kindness to the poor, the establishment of social gospel and even church membership itself. Remember, not even our very best can be good enough for God—He is righteous and holy!

There it is. Faith! Nothing more nothing less! Have you put your faith and trust in the Lord Jesus?

It is like a little child standing on the edge of a swimming pool. In the water with his arms outstretched is Daddy. Holding his breath while closing his eyes, the child jumps. He knows that Daddy will not let him down. That is trust. Jesus will not let you down. Trust in Him by faith!

Salvation belongs to our God. The Bible is clear at this point. "For we maintain that a man is justified by faith apart from observing the law" (Ro 3:28). The result is justification. It is "just as if we have never sinned!" This is accomplished through faith.

A summary of the four requirements for salvation might be helpful.
1. Repent of your sin
2. Confess your sin to the Lord Jesus Christ
3. Believe in your heart that God raised Jesus from the dead
4. Trust in Him by faith

CHAPTER THREE

Confused Feelings

"I feel good!"
— James Brown

Outside of salvation, I do not believe that there is a more serious question than, "How do I know, for sure, that I am totally secure?" This question is asked by scores of men and women who struggle with the issue of their total security. Many people who have repented of their sin, confessed to Jesus Christ, believe in the resurrection and have trusted by faith lead defeated and dejected lives because they ride a spiritual rollercoaster. At times they feel saved, all is well, life is good. The preacher is on track, stocks are up, the kids are growing well, the sun is shining. How easy, in a sense, to feel saved when life is good!

Here's the problem. Life is simply not one continuous mountaintop experience. Few people genuinely stay happy all the time. Yet many believe that anything less than a happy smile all day is evidence of ingratitude towards God- perhaps even somewhat "unchristian." The abundant life of Christ (Jo 10:10), they believe, demands a perpetual positive attitude. Anything less is a betrayal of the joy which Christ gives to His children.

Worship leaders often reinforce this uncomfortable dichotomy between human emotions and spiritual propriety. It is not uncommon to hear the phrase "Let's all stand with smiles on our faces and greet each other with the love of the Lord this morning!" Yet this denies the realities of life. One of my mentors in the ministry, Cecil Randall, reminded his seminary students of the reality that, "There's a broken heart on every pew!"

If simply feeling good and smiling all day was enough to guarantee my eternal security, I would be in serious trouble. It is well nigh impossible to feel good all the time, let alone to smile all the day long.

Surely such an attitude has overlooked the life of the Lord Jesus Christ. Here we have "the spotless Lamb of God" bound up in a human body. This is the One who loved us so that much that He was willing to reduce Himself to a human egg. The Immaculate Conception was not just about the epitome of love and grace, it was about the willingness of the Son to travel the journey of human experience.

Here we have Our Savior from the cradle to the cross. Look at the baby when Mary's time to deliver had come. Observe the pain of the birth canal and the embarrassing slap on the bottom designed to produce the first yell of life. Imagine the scream from the little fellow's lungs as his father cut his umbilical cord.

Writhe in pain with the little Jewish lad as He is circumcised on the eighth day according to the custom of His people. Consider the pain of His childhood as the little boy trips and falls after learning to take His first step.

Take a peek into the carpenter's shop where it would be unthinkable for the son not to have experimented with his father's tools. Imagine the pain of a misguided hammer, the stab of a sharp point, the countless numbers of splinters embedded deep in His hands.

Confused Feelings

Journey with our Lord down the highway of life that led Him to the cross:

See Him as He begins His ministry. He had become "flesh and dwelt among us" (Jn 1:14).

Watch Him explode with anger at the Passover time when, upon entry into the temple, He found "those who sold oxen and sheep and doves, and the money changers doing business" (Jn 2:14).

Watch the concern on the faces of the disciples because their Master was hungry. Observe Him as He walks for miles and miles on dirt tracks and small pathways with nothing but a pair of hand-made sandals that would cause any Nike manufacturer to laugh with scorn.

Stand next to the Son of Man as the Sadducees and Pharisees hurled insult after insult at Him.

Watch how tired and weary He became as He poured out His life into a bunch of bewildered men.

Walk alongside Him as He mingled among the masses on hillsides while observing their hunger and desperation.

Feel the agonizing expression of love for Lazarus—heartfelt because Lazarus was His friend, heart-sore because His friends were so devastated, and hopeful because He was capable of raising a dead man from the grave.

Hear Jesus cry out in response to the Pharisees' reluctance to confess their faith for fear that they would be put out of the Synagogue.

Sail with Him as He sets out for the other side of the Sea of Galilee in order to try and escape the tension of an overbearing crowd.

Examine the agony of His soul as He approaches His hour of destiny. Turn away in disbelief as the hysteria of the crowd reaches a thunderous demand for blood. Stagger into the hallway as you watch the vicious slapping of the cat o' nine tails ripping flesh out of His back time and time again like a rabid lion mounted on the back of a helpless deer, his fangs ripping out chunks of raw meat.

Listen to the horrible orchestra of laughing soldiers who mocked and hurled insults; step out onto the *via delorosa* down the highway to the cross. Step by step, shuffle by shuffle. Every bone, every sinew racked in pain. Twisting, turning, burning, sweat pouring, eyes glazing. Masses of screaming people—hoards of them—clamoring for a glimpse of the best show in town on Friday morning. There they are running, clapping, jeering, spitting, crowding, desperate to tell their children that they were there.

Feel the horror of the first nail ripping through His body. Jerk upright when the cross is hoisted and dropped into the hole that receives its unlikely cargo like a vacuum cleaner sucking up the dirt on a filthy carpet. Yell out in indescribable pain as every joint and ligament is contorted and ripped out of line as our Savior is set to stand in ignominious shame between two horrid thieves who deserved to die.

So, you feel saved, do you? If the Son of God writhed in pain and wept; if the spotless Lamb of God begged the Father to deliver Him from the cross; if our Lord Jesus Christ suffered the rigors reserved for the frailty of our human predicament, how much more so should we who are "yet with sin."

Imagine going up to an expectant mother about to deliver a baby. Try telling her how good she looks or, better yet, ask her if she feels totally secure at that point.

I remember well the day one of our sons was born. Up early in the morning, we rushed to the Baptist Hospital in New Orleans. The hour had come. After nearly 17 hours of labor my wife was in no condition to be pampered, patronized, played with or poked fun at! Can you imagine me walking up to her at such a critical moment and saying something like, "Honey, do you feel saved right now?" I would probably be better off spending 10 years on death row than suffer the consequences of such a stupid question!

Think about these things. If the total security of my salvation were dependant on my feelings, what hope would I ever have? My feelings are connected to the roller coaster of my human emotions. They bounce around, they run the gauntlet of life, tripping, bumping, fracturing, struggling.

Our emotions remind me of a surfer perched on a surfboard. The platform provides the foundation upon which he stands. The day is gorgeous, the sea spectacular. The swell of a wave begins to draw like the early signs of a pending yawn. Before long a massive mountain of water presents itself in heart-stopping splendor. He paddles furiously, and then jumps in elation to ride the elevated throne of his lofty kingdom. The world lies at his feet. He zips and careens down the slippery slope of the curling wave. A moment of true ecstasy. Behind him looms the menace of sudden interruption.

As though exhausted, the wave readies itself to capitulate. Like the snarling curled lip of a warthog, the wave bears down on the surfer. With finality, it crashes down on his head with venom that would make a spitting cobra proud! Despite all his expertise he cannot stay bolted to his perch. He becomes consumed, rolled around, thumped on the bottom of the ocean one minute and thrown into the coral reef the next. He gasps for air. His lungs cry out for anything that has breath.

Finally, life has passed between his ears and despair has settled into silent acceptance. Then, without notice or fanfare, an upward swirl of a cross current catapults him toward the surface of the sea. His face breaks through like a groundhog emerging from a long winter. His mouth and nose suck deep as though to drain the very essence of the breath God breathed into the nostrils of man.

Sheer exhaustion leaves him collapsed on a desolate beach. Nothing but a broken surfboard and a dazed look remain for this one-time gallant warrior!

Such is life. Such are our emotions!

Never base the fact of salvation on feelings. Total security comes from the heart of God, not the feelings of man.

I am forgiven because I repented of my sin. I am released from the bondage of Satan because I confessed my sin to the Lord Jesus Christ. I am a Christian because I am convinced in my heart that God raised Jesus from the dead. I am born again because I put my faith and trust in the Savior of the world. I am totally secure because the Bible tells me I can be.

Do not misunderstand at this point. The life of Christ is "an abundant life" (Jn 10:10). Nothing can compare to knowing the Lord Jesus Christ as personal Savior. He is the closest friend ever. The joy of knowing that all sin has been forgiven is unsurpassed. This is a full and meaningful life. The peace of God, "which surpasses all understanding" (Phil. 4), is made available to all believers through Jesus Christ, our Lord. "Therefore, if anyone is in Christ, he is a new creation; old things have passed away; behold, all things have become new" (2 Cor. 5:17).

The greater question is whether or not I have truly been saved to begin with.

CHAPTER FOUR

Making Contact

*"I want you to know
that I am a born-again Christian"*
— President George W. Bush

It is at this point that we must examine our own hearts before the Lord. This can only be done in the light of His Word.

Here we must take a stand. I do not believe that the Bible contains the Word of the Lord: I believe it *is* the Word of God. What good would any study of the Scriptures be if any part of it was called into question? From Genesis to Revelation we hear God's full and complete revelation of Himself through His Son. The Bible is without any mixture of error and is totally and completely reliable as complete and utter truth. As such, it is the infallible Word of the Living God. All we need to know about God, His love toward us and our reconciliation to Him, is found in the pages of this wonderful book. Inspired by the Holy Spirit, every word is infallible because it is God-breathed.

Because of this we must turn to the only source of our total security. What does the Bible have to say about this extremely critical issue?

I remember making a visit with a pastor while preaching a revival series in his church. The home we entered was under the command of a rather arrogant man who made no bones about his disdain for Christianity, and also hated preachers! Shortly after introductions were made, the pastor attempted to read the Scriptures to him. I would rather not describe the words this man used to express his intense dislike for the Word of God.

What surprised me was the response of the pastor. "Well, Sir, if you are not willing to hear what the Bible has to say, then I regret to inform you that I have nothing else to say to you!" We were immediately evicted.

Two nights later, following the evening service in which many came to know the Lord Jesus as their personal Savior, I found myself shaking hands at the door of the church. A man standing in the shadows came to my attention. It was the same young man! Shortly after he gave his heart and life to Jesus I asked him: "My friend, why did you come here tonight after being so adamant about your hatred of God and His Word?" His reply was deliberate and forthright. The "nothing else to say outside of God's Word" statement made by the pastor had left the man reeling in desperate consternation. God had his attention. Salvation has nothing to do with the opinion of man. It is exclusive to our Lord!

Are you willing to trust the matter of your total security to human feelings or to the Living Word of our Living God? In the next chapters the five "acid tests" of salvation will be developed and explained. Write them in the portals of your heart.

I will promise you this for sure. If you can affirm these five truths in application to your own relationship with the Lord Jesus Christ, you are totally secure. Three prerequisites however, are essential before this study begins.

Prerequisite 1

Seek God's Face in Prayer

Ask the Lord Jesus to reveal the truth of His Word to you through His Holy Spirit. If you are indeed saved and secure, one of the first signs of confirmation will become evident through this process. Only a person who has a personal relationship with the Lord Jesus will hear and understand the things which God has to say. This comes through the indwelling presence of the Holy Spirit in the life of every believer.

Mary came to this understanding after a long struggle in her spiritual life. For many years she endured one hardship after another. She had little trouble remembering the tent crusade held by her church every year. The preacher went on and on about it. Special people were selected to do special things for special nights during which special emphases were made. Each service was preceded by a dinner on the grounds. Food flowed in abundance and even "the grumpy old deacons" put on a show for the guest evangelist. Everyone, according to Mary, put "their best foot forward" during the annual revival.

Youth night was always on the final night of the crusade. Mary was there because it was the right thing to do based on her parents' opinion. But she was really there for the boys. Mary had no trouble "going down front" with all the others. The girls usually "went down" together and their "going down" was accompanied by much wailing and sorrow for all the unmentionable thoughts and things girls just ought not to indulge in.

By the age of 20, Mary was married with a baby on the way. Her husband was immature and abusive and soon walked out on her for another girl much prettier than his young wife. By the age of 35 or so, when I met her, Mary had been through every conceivable hurt and pain imaginable. All she had to hold on to was a decision that she had made years earlier.

Every service of the crusade in which I was preaching concluded with Mary, down front, on her knees, weeping. The pastor asked me to speak to her. Evidently Mary was well known for her rapid and frequent response at the end of most of the church worship services—even on regular Sundays.

I took a passage from the Bible and asked her to read it to me and the pastor. She did in a broken and searching voice. But when I asked her to tell me what it meant she told me that she had no earthly idea.

And so, laying aside all other matters, I asked Mary if she would give her heart and life to Jesus. Right there, on the front pew of the church, Mary repented, confessed, believed in her heart that God had raised Jesus from the dead, and put her faith and trust in Him. When she opened her eyes I asked her to read the same passage that I had previously asked her to read. This time her eyes sparkled as she exclaimed, "Oh, I see what that means now!"

What had happened? What was the difference between the first and second readings of the same passage from the Bible? The difference was the presence of the Holy Spirit. No matter what decision Mary had taken in prior years, no matter how many times she had "walked the aisle" or "gone down front" or raised her hand in response to a prayer, Mary had never met the Lord Jesus Christ. And, as we will see more clearly in a later chapter, if Jesus Christ has not come into your heart, the Holy Spirit has not come into your heart. And if the Holy Spirit has not come into your heart, it is impossible to understand the truth of the Word of God. An important function of the Holy Spirit is to guide you into truth and to help you to see and understand the mysteries of the deep and wonderful things about God.

So, it follows that Mary underwent a change. She met Jesus. He came into her heart. And when He came into her heart along, came the Holy Spirit, who is God Himself.

Seek God's face in prayer. Do it now. Your total security may be in place already! Only a true believer will understand the things of God. For only a believer is indwelt by God's Holy Spirit.

Prerequisite 2

Open The Scriptures And Read Them Personally

I pray that I, as author of this book, will be an instrument in the hands of the Lord Jesus; but I have nothing to say outside the Word of God. Neither the National Geographic nor a local newspaper can ever be used as an authority when it comes to one's relationship with God. God's Word is the lamp and light. So, open your Bible personally. It will unlock the key to being totally secure.

The Word of God is living and active. Sharper than any double-edged sword, it penetrates even to

> dividing soul and spirit, joints and marrow; it judges the thoughts and attitudes of the heart. Nothing in all creation is hidden from God's sight. Everything is uncovered and laid bare before the eyes of Him to whom we must give an account.
> — *Hebrews 4:12-13 (NIV)*

For many months Frank just sat in church and listened. His face bore little expression. For a serious-minded businessman, this seemed quite natural. One day he asked me to pay him a visit. In his office I asked him to give his heart and life to the Lord Jesus Christ. He replied that he had done so and was confident of the fact. I had no reason to doubt him. Then he began to share with me the struggle he was having with total security.

"How could anyone be sure?" he questioned. "Surely no man but God Himself can ever really know."

I tried to explain that the act of salvation is something that only God can do. Only God can save. Only Jesus can forgive. Yes, a man's salvation is a private matter between himself and his God, but not so his Christianity. A man's Christianity is the public outworking of his salvation. While works cannot save a man, faith without works is dead. And so, I informed my friend, there is no such thing as "a secret service agent in the kingdom of God."

"Read it for yourself and you will see," I pointed out.

Today, as I preach the Word of God, Frank sits there with his Bible wide open on his lap. The constant smile on his face is a joy to behold!

Prerequisite 3

Trust The Lord Jesus To Open Your Heart

Please understand how significant this is. Nothing could be more important than knowing that your sins have been forgiven. One day, when death comes, or if the Lord Jesus were to come back before your death, you will be transported instantly into heaven. The next chapters will present you with the facts from the Bible. Ask the Lord to open your heart to receive His truth. He will do so if you ask this of Him.

As we present the truth of God's Word, two things will happen:

A) *Biblical Confirmation.* God will confirm the fact of your salvation through His Word and by His Spirit. You will be able to confirm and affirm the reality of each one of these five truths as they apply to your own life. You will be able to apply truth in the sense that if the shoe fits you will be able to wear it. As such you will find yourself totally secure. The joy of knowing for sure is essential to one's walk with the Lord.

B) *Personal Acceptance.* Be prepared to accept the fact that you may be living in a fool's paradise. It is, after all, possible to have "walked down the aisle," lifted a hand in response to an invitation, or even said a prayer, but still not be saved. Neither church membership nor baptism can save anyone. Jesus is the only way. Please hear this clearly.

Many people have become "casualties" of modern day evangelism. The insatiable clamor to have good statistics, bragging rights, and the football coach philosophy of "win at all costs" has, sadly, filled many churches with people masquerading as Christians. "Easy believism" has infiltrated the evangelical church at an alarming rate. Disunity in congregations, ungodly behavior among church leaders, disloyalty from staff members, shallowness in the pulpit and the ruined witness of the church are just a few obvious consequences produced by unsaved church members.

It is imperative to grapple with the truth of God's Word. I beg you to answer these questions before the Lord Jesus. Should you be unable to affirm any one of these truths, you are neither forgiven nor saved for all time and eternity. You are not totally secure. In fact, should this be true of you, you are not secure at all. And, as we will soon discover, there is no such thing as "sort of secure" or "maybe secure" or "I just hope so" kind of secure. According to God's Word, you are either for or against the Lord Jesus. No man can serve God and man. Do something about this immediately.

The final pages will give clear instructions from the Bible on how to know for sure whether you are saved. Contrary to public opinion, you can be totally secure.

One more word before we dive headlong into these five "acid tests" of our salvation. Many people, such as parents, have indicated great concern for family members. Many are able to testify to the very moment when their child made a public profession of faith—perhaps at camp, during a crusade or while kneeling at a bedside. Since then, however, the child's life has been on a downward spiral, spiritually speaking. Years later, little evidence can be provided concerning this person's relationship with Jesus Christ. Is this person saved or not? How does the fact of "once saved, always saved" apply?

Listen carefully! "Once saved, always saved" is the wrong question. God has settled this issue. If God has saved you, you are "washed and redeemed by the blood of the Lamb."

Peter puts it this way:

> For you know that it was not with perishable things such as silver and gold that you were redeemed from the empty way of life handed down to you from your forefathers, but with the precious blood of Christ, a lamb without blemish or defect.
> — *1 Peter 1: 18-19 (NIV)*

The more important question concerns the reality of one's salvation to begin with. Was this person, indeed, saved when the decision was made? Did he meet the Savior and enter into a personal one-on-one relationship with Him? A major reason why so many are not totally secure is because of this fact. Security can never be achieved in the heart of a person when The Securer has never entered his or her heart. His name is Jesus Christ, and He is the only one capable of securing the hearts of people like you and me for all time and for all eternity.

I have always been fascinated by sheep. During many of my university vacations in Africa I found myself employed on farms. One, in particular, was magnificent. The farm itself stretched for miles and miles, and part of my responsibility was to help supervise the welfare of over 40,000 sheep. We herded them, inoculated them, sheared them, slaughtered them and ate them!

Sheep need a shepherd—they depend on him. Without him, they hurt themselves; they get lost; wild animals gain access to them and kill them. They become as dumb as dumb can possibly be.

During my adventure days in Africa my brother, Rod, and I came careening around a mountain pass in a remote part of Africa on his huge BSA 650 Thunderbolt motorcycle and almost ended up killing ourselves because of sheep—dumb sheep without a shepherd! Hundreds of them were grazing on the left side of the highway. The roar of the motorcycle, miles from civilization, startled them. The one nearest the road looked up in horror as we came around the corner, both leaning far to the left with our legs almost touching the ground, and began to trot across the road directly in front of us. Guess what the remaining sheep did? They followed right behind, and soon sheep filled every inch of the roadway in front of us. Only the quick reflexes of my oldest brother averted a disaster!

Here's the issue: When Jesus was on earth He had to deal with many people who claimed to be righteous. They claimed to know God. They shoved their "religiosity" and their "churchiosity" and their laws down Jesus' throat as they challenged His every claim to be the Messiah.

On one of those occasions these people gathered around Him and demanded that He show them proof of His identity. In John 10: 25-30 Jesus answered:

> "I told you, and you do not believe. The works that I do in My Father's name, they bear witness of Me. But you do not believe, because you are not of My sheep, as I said to you. My sheep hear My voice, and I know them, and they follow Me. And I give them eternal life, and they shall never perish; neither shall

anyone snatch them out of My hand. My Father, who
has given them to Me, is greater than all; and no one
is able to snatch them out of My Father's hand. I and
My Father are one."

Wow! Did you get it? When you believe, you become one of God's sheep, and once you have become one of His sheep no one can pluck you out of His hand! Now that's total security!

And a sheep never has to prove that it is a sheep! Just watch it behave. If someone claims to have given his heart and life to Jesus, surely something ought to be there as proof. There is no such thing as "a secret service agent" in the Kingdom of God! Salvation is private in that only the Lord Jesus can save a lost person. God, in His sovereign grace, made the provision for our salvation through the death of His Son, the Lord Jesus Christ, on the cross.

But the outworking evidence of salvation is plain for everyone to see. Jesus reminded us of this fact when He used the analogy of a candle being lighted. What good is a lighted candle if it is hidden? Looking from the shores of the Sea of Galilee, Jesus pointed out the city of Safed set up on a hillside. How can a city set up on a hill be hidden from view, he asked of His disciples?

The Bible teaches clearly that "fruit" is an essential mark of a believer. As Paul wrote to the church in Galatia:

But the fruit of the Spirit is love, joy, peace, patience,
kindness, goodness, faithfulness, gentleness and self-
control. Against such there is no law. Those who
belong to Christ have crucified the sinful nature with

> its passions and desires. Since we live by the Spirit, let us keep in step with the Spirit.
> — *Galatians 5:22-25 (NIV)*

God's Word leaves no room for debate at this point. In other words, a person who claims to know Christ as personal Lord and Savior and yet demonstrates little change, more than likely, has never met the Lord Jesus.

One of the most powerful images I have of this very issue was presented to me while traveling across Australia some years ago. My wife, Karyn, and I found ourselves privileged to be leading a mission in the great city of Brisbane in Queensland. Much preparation had been done but much of the leadership were generally skeptical. They told me that they had a particular problem with what they referred to as "American style" invitations at the end of the crusade services.

With a tender and understanding heart I explained to them just how important it was to give people an opportunity to respond, publicly, to the voice of God. After all, I pointed out, Jesus could have arranged a private execution if He had been so inclined. Being God, He could easily have ordered His own death down some quiet alleyway in Jerusalem so that few, if any, would have had to actually see the Son of Man die in such a horrid fashion. He could have easily arranged for the disciples to discover His lifeless body at a later time.

But He did not. The Son of Man was fully obedient to the Father. His impending suffering was as real to Him as suffering is to you and me. Remember, Jesus was both fully God and fully man. He knows what it is to hurt and struggle because He hurt and struggled.

You may remember how Jesus pleaded with the Father in the

Garden of Gethsemane to "take the cup" away from Him. This was the cup of His pain and suffering. But He accepted the will of God the Father. Right there in the garden. Knowing full and well what lay ahead of Him. Excruciating pain and suffering. Public humiliation of the highest order.

I explained all this to the leadership in Brisbane, Australia. They listened with reluctant interest, chatted among themselves and then allowed me to ask those present to stand up and step out publicly and do what God was telling them to do.

My message that night was the same message of hope for all people. It centered squarely on the Lord Jesus Christ. Using the Bible, I told the crowd that Jesus is the only one who can forgive our sin, the only one who came make us brand new, and the only one who can give us hope beyond the grave.

I did not know that Harold was there. I had never met Harold, but what I did not know was that this middle-aged man had come to the crusade with great reluctance. He told me after the meeting of his anger and of his dysfunctional and selfish life. God took a hold of him that night.

Scores and scores of people were moved to respond to the gospel invitation. Harold found himself in a state of nervous and confused perplexion. He wanted to step out and come but his pride held him back. He wrestled and fought in his heart. He knew about God in his head. He had heard all about Jesus during his youth. He had attended many a church service and had made quite a few decisions. But, he told me later, there was no evidence, no security.

Harold came forward that night to receive the Lord Jesus into his heart and life. I believe that Harold met Jesus that night in Brisbane. His life would never be the same. He became one of Christ's sheep.

Even though I have never seen nor heard from Harold again since that night, I truly believe that no one and nothing in this world can ever pluck him out of the hand of the Great Shepherd of the sheep. Now that's total security!

Such is the theme of this book. How can we know, for certain, if we are saved? If not by virtue of what we feel, then by what means? Where do we go to find the answers?

We will consult the Word of God, the Bible. And, as we do so, five major questions will be presented to us. They will be asked individually and personally.

The Lord Jesus called a meeting of His disciples in Matthew 16:13-20. Everybody was talking about Him. Everyone had an opinion. All the people were asking questions. In today's world the talk shows would have been buzzing.

It was the same way when the devastation caused by the Tsunami in Asia in the winter of 2005 left the world in a state of profound shock and dismay. Hundreds of thousands of people lost their lives and many more found themselves devastated beyond human reason. While coalitions of the world's armies still debate the merits of a united effort to rid the world of despots and dictators, it took less than a few weeks for the world to come together in a massive outpouring of compassion and practical aid for the victims of such a catastrophe. But the religious debate was another thing entirely. In the United States, Larry King Live was but one of many who brought religious leaders to discuss and espouse the merits of God's involvement in all of this. Consensus was sought but never found.

Such was the case as it unfolded before the disciples who stood before the Lord Jesus to answer one of the most soul-searching questions ever asked. Right there, at Caesarea Philippi, Jesus put his finger on the issue.

"Who do people say the Son of Man is?" Jesus asked His disciples. His band of followers had little difficulty in their response. Some believed this and others believed that, they answered. Some said that Jesus was none other than John the Baptist, while others believed that He was one of the prophets. The court of public opinion was certainly no different to our own day and age. Just watch television, listen to the radio, tune in to some religious broadcasting, walk the streets and knock on a few doors, or take a survey.

This is where Jesus challenged them. "But what about you?" the Savior asked. "Who do *you* say that I am?"

Peter had no problem in confessing that he believed Jesus was the Christ, the Son of the living God. What about you?

You can be totally secure if you are able to answer these five questions before the Lord. Remember, this is not about your parents, your church, public opinion or a feeling you may or may not have. This is about you and your relationship with the Lord Jesus Christ.

These are the five questions which must be answered before the Lord:

1. Am I sensitive to sin?
2. Am I submissive to God's commandments?
3. Am I saturated in God's love?
4. Am I Spirit filled?
5. Am I Scripturally convinced?

Have an open copy of the Bible with you. Turn to the first letter to John which you will find near the end of the New Testament. The next five chapters of this book will help develop a firm understanding of God's mandate concerning the vital matter of your total security.

Your life will never be the same. You will be set free. Your confidence level will rise dramatically. You will become even more productive in your daily life and, especially, in your spiritual service. You will have a far greater sense of God's purpose for you. You will be able to help others in a significant way. You will see and understand sin in a totally new light, both in your own life and also, in the lives of others around you. You will see all the things going on in our troubled world through the eyes of God and you will be able to interpret even the catastrophes of life in the light of God's perspective. You will relate to your children from a spiritual perspective and you will understand their struggles and behavior patterns in a totally meaningful way. You will be able to pray for your children and those you love, and you will relate to them in a far more meaningful way.

You will know what lies beneath. You will face even death will absolute certainty and total God-given serenity. You will change from a pebble in the sand to a rock on the mountain side. You will quit wandering and begin standing still . Instead of sitting down you will stand up. And instead of just standing up you will become the one who steps out.

You will be the salt of the earth! You will change from being an "I think so" sort of Christian to an "I know so" solid Christian! You will become dependable, confident, responsible, bold and certain of who you are. You will become totally secure!

CHAPTER FIVE

Am I Sensitive to Sin?

*"If we say that we have no sin,
we deceive ourselves, and the truth is not in us."*
— 1 John 1:8

Our study will focus on the first letter written by John. It may be helpful to remember that the New Testament has four Books by John. One "big" John, which is the fourth Gospel in addition to Matthew, Mark and Luke; then, at the end of the New Testament just before Jude and Revelation, we find three "little" Johns, all of which are letters or epistles.

A closer look at the meaning of the text is imperative if we are to understand its full meaning and impact. Note that it begins with a clearly stated condition. The little word "if" is very important as we will soon see.

In this passage, John tells us that our relationship with Jesus Christ, who is truth, is impossible if we "claim to be without sin." It follows that such a person most certainly does not have security, since the means by which total security is tested is the question of sin.

The writer leaves no room for discussion at this point. Many parents understand the nature and intent of a conditional statement. "Son, if you do not shut that television set off now, and go and do your homework, you will not be going to the prom!" It's amazing how quickly homework can be done. Once applied, sons and daughters understand the meaning of a conditional statement too!

Athletes run plays frequently on conditional circumstances. The coach determines his next move based on the move the opposition makes. If they do this, then we do that. One of the most successful college football coaches is Steve Spurrier. His tenure with the Florida Gators was marked by one victory after another. His teams were always a threat. When Danny Weurfel won the coveted Heisman Trophy, the Gators were unstoppable.

One of the marks of the genius of Spurrier's offense, I am told, was his ability to change the play at the line of scrimmage at a split second's notice. A former Heisman quarterback himself, Spurrier had the ability to read defensive posturing moments before the ball was snapped. His quarterback would receive the signaled change of play from his head coach, step back into the pocket and brilliantly out-maneuver the opposition. These plays were determined by a condition—the "if" dictated the result.

Here, in 1 John 1:8, the condition is clear. The condition, in fact, is a driving incentive to examine its meaning. This is very personal. You and I have to come to grips with this. If my attitude to sin has a direct impact on my total security, then I want to know exactly what is meant by the claim to " be without sin."

It is also very important to realize that this is written to people who professed to be Christians. The "we" refers to those who had, at some

Am I Sensitive to Sin?   55

time or another, made their profession of faith in Christ. Perhaps the United States is smitten by the "royal we" as much as any nation in the world. Proportionately, "we" are a nation "under God." This God is none other than the God and Father of our Lord Jesus Christ. Our founding fathers left no room for doubt in this regard. Many regard the United States to be a Christian country. Thousands, if not millions, take license in that they have been born and reared in a Christian country. In some parts of the deep South few would claim not to believe in God. Most citizens acknowledge God in one way or another.

This was the problem with a highly educated man by the name of Nicodemus who had an encounter with Jesus. In John 2:23 and following, it is clear that the basis for the belief of many during Jesus' time was the miracles and signs which they had seen the Savior doing. The crowds had watched as Jesus did amazing things, such as making blind people see again and lame people walk again. What they saw with their eyes made it easy for them to believe with their heads.

I recall a lady once telling me that she was a Christian because she belonged to a certain church. Belonging to a church is very important. It is, in fact, indispensable for a believer. But "just because you are born in a car-port does not make you a motor car!"

Here we learn a stark truth about our total security. Being totally secure is not about what we see in order to believe. Being totally secure is not about where we were born or what we have done to educate ourselves.

So here are all these people who "claim" to know Christ because they have witnessed the miracles He has done. One of the most striking of all passages follows in the next two verses when we read, "but Jesus did not trust Himself to them, for He knew all men. He did not need man's testimony about man, for He knew what was in man."

The dramatic encounter that takes place in the next few verses is intended to illustrate this predicament. Nicodemus was imminently qualified to be a Christian—from a human perspective. He had spent many years studying religion, had become a leading cleric, and was highly respected as a religious leader. Furthermore, he had no problem in recognizing Jesus for the miracles He had performed and the good work He had done.

But he was not a Christian! One can only imagine the shock when Jesus said to him, "You [Nicodemus] must be born again!" The text that we are dealing with is talking about all people who categorize themselves as believers but who are deceived in thinking so. So-called Christians who are masquerading as such are exposed.

The central issue is sin. Evidently, some of the people listening to Jesus claimed to be "without sin." How can these things be? Listen carefully lest your misconception condemn you to a fool's paradise. All human beings are "born in sin." Paul emphasized this in his letter to the people at Rome:

As it is written:

> "There is none righteous, no, not one;
> There is none who understands;
> There is none who seeks after God.
> They have all turned aside;
> They have together become unprofitable;
> There is none who does good, no, not one."
> "Their throat is an open tomb;
> With their tongues they have practiced deceit",
> The poison of asps is under their lips",

> "Whose mouth is full of cursing and bitterness."
> "Their feet are swift to shed blood;
> Destruction and misery are in their ways;
> And the way of peace they have not known."
> "There is no fear of God before their eyes."
> — *Romans 3:10-18*

So, here it is. If those of us who claim to be Christians deny our own sinfulness, then we must accept the consequences.

Let's deal, first of all, with the matter of denial. Is this something we say or is it, perhaps, an action or way of life? Or is this related to some specific incident or event? While all of the above are relevant, saying that we have no sin addresses the issue of our attitude toward sin.

Put more bluntly, does sin bother me? When I sin does it trouble me? Please note that the operative word here is not "if" I sin, but "when." The Bible teaches that we are sinners by nature and by choice. In fact, the Psalmist reminds us that we are "conceived in sin." Paul confirms this by telling us that "all have sinned and fallen short of the glory of God." When Christ comes into my heart and life I am most assuredly forgiven of all my sin, once and for all!

But I do not become immune from sin. Paul wrestled with his sinful condition time without number and cried out in frustration and desperation to the Lord:

> For what I am doing, I do not understand. For what I will to do, that I do not practice; but what I hate, that I do. If, then, I do what I will not to do, I agree with the law that it is good. But now, it is no longer I who do it,

> but sin that dwells in me. For I know that in me (that is, in my flesh) nothing good dwells; for to will is present with me, but how to perform what is good I do not find. For the good that I will to do, I do not do; but the evil I will not to do, that I practice. Now if I do what I will not to do, it is no longer I who do it, but sin that dwells in me.
>
> I find then a law, that evil is present with me, the one who wills to do good. For I delight in the law of God according to the inward man. But I see another law in my members, warring against the law of my mind, and bringing me into captivity to the law of sin which is in my members. O wretched man that I am! Who will deliver me from this body of death? I thank God—through Jesus Christ our Lord!
>
> So then, with the mind I myself serve the law of God, but with the flesh the law of sin.
>
> —*Romans 7:15-25*

Having my sin forgiven cannot be confused with exemption from sin. Besides the devil prowls around like a roaring lion looking for humans to destroy and devour. We are prime candidates! How can I be exempt from sin when only the Lord Jesus is perfect? Some may misconstrue the forgiveness we have in the Lord Jesus as an excuse to pursue sin. Perhaps God's grace carries automatic coverage? God forbid!

Sensitivity to sin, then, is the core issue. It is not a matter of whether or not I am immune or exempt from sin, but does sin bother me at all? Herein lies an acid-test of my salvation. In fact, John gives us a peek into the ministry of the Holy Spirit at this point. We will come back to this matter in another chapter. But it must be noted that the only means by which a person is able to be sensitized to sin is by the indwelling presence of the Holy Spirit. His work is to counteract the appearance and threat of sin in the life of every believer. In other words, when sin makes even the slightest effort to penetrate the life of a believer, the Holy Spirit jumps into action. Brakes are applied with full force! The itch begins. Turmoil reigns. Sin must and will trouble a believer—and, because it does so, we will soon see this is a major source of total security.

The presence of sin in my life should never be construed as a sign of my lack of total security. The fact that I want to sin, and that I do sin, does not in any way affect my total security. Rather, it is my attitude toward and my recognition of the sin in my life that guarantees my total security. I know this sounds awfully strange. At face value, and with a rush to judgment, someone reading this could jump to the conclusion that this is providing a case for the celebration of sin. After all, since the Lord Jesus has taken our sin away and cast it all as "far as the east is from the west to remember it no more," this must that mean you and I should enjoy our sin. Why worry about it when it's all forgiven?

No, my friend, this is not about celebrating sin. It's about attitude toward sin. It's about identifying what it is. It's about doing something about it.

I remember playing the English sport of cricket as a young man. I still love the game and every visit to the shores of England, South Africa, Australia and New Zealand is always accompanied by frequent trips to a cricket ground for a refresher course. Just before taking my turn "at bat" my stomach would churn with nerves. We called this phenomenon having "butterflies in our stomachs." In fact, butterflies were considered a good thing to have and experience. They served notice. They prevented pride coming before a fall. They helped focus attention on the matter at hand. They kept the mighty humble. They served to remind the batsman to invoke all the skills necessary to succeed at what he was about to do. This would include all the defensive measures and strategies that he had been taught to prevent him from being given out without having made a single contribution to his team's score. Butterflies warned him of the impending danger. A skillful bowler was ready to get him out!

Many a cricketer with potential never rose to any greatness in his art because he refused to recognize or acknowledge his need. My lesson on this matter came during a stint in the army. Apparently my cricketing ability was recognized the day that our unit of candidate officers played a friendly against the hated unit of "para-bats." Colonel Rensberg was so impressed that he sent me to the capital city to play in the trial matches for potential selection to the national armed forces team. Expectations were high as this young officer, clad in the all-white uniform of a proper cricketer, strolled out to the "pitch" to take strike. The bowler, who went by the name of "spook" or "ghost," came thundering down the runway to let rip with a near hundred mile-an-hour fast ball at this over-confident, well hyped-up young player. Three balls later I was on my way back to the pavilion with one of my wickets ripped unceremoniously out of its place and deposited some way down the field.

My problem was that I claimed to be without fear. I refused to recognize my weaknesses. I paid the price! I never made the national team.

So it is with many who claim to be Christians but refuse to say that they have any sin. The presence, potential, and even appearance of sin in a person's life should provide the "butterflies" that sound the alarm, not only in regards to the consequences of sin, but in terms of a confirmation of that person's total security. If you have no "butterflies"— if sin does not make you uncomfortable—it may well indicate that the Holy Spirit is not present in your life. If that is the case, then you are not born again to begin with. Claiming to be without sin for a person who thinks that he's saved is like batting without "butterflies" for a cricketer. You will never make God's "national" team.

Let's go the other way around. Recognition of sin means that you acknowledge the presence of sin in your life. Acknowledging sin means that you are troubled by its presence in your life. Being troubled by sin means that the Holy Spirit is active in your life. The presence of the Holy Spirit means the presence of truth. Presence of truth means the presence of Jesus. The presence of Jesus means salvation. Salvation means total security!

The Apostle John pulls no punches. He puts it on the line. No recognition of personal sin, no Christian. No sensitivity, no salvation. How do we come to such a conclusion? Surely this is judgmental? What right does any person have to judge another? After all, only God knows who truly has been converted. These points are true, but just as the evidence of a fruit tree is the fruit it bears, so it is with those of us who profess to be saved people.

Watch how John puts this all into perspective. "If we say we have no sin, we deceive ourselves and the truth is not in us." The people who claim to have no sin suffer two major consequences:

1. They Will Live A Life of Deceit.

As such their Christian claim is nothing more than a masquerade. It is false. It is not genuine. It is non-existent. It never happened.

2. They Will Have No Security.

Put bluntly, the truth is not in them. So, how could they possibly have any security, let alone total security? Once again we rely on the evidence of Scripture. When Jesus was preparing His disciples for His imminent death and subsequent departure back into heaven, He made the critical point of saying in John 14:6, "I am the way, the truth, and the life. No one comes to the Father except through me."

Jesus is the only way to the Father, Jesus is truth, and a person who says that he has no sin does not have truth in him. It follows then that such a one is not saved. No truth, no Jesus, no salvation, no security!

Let me illustrate. Many years ago I preached the gospel in a city church at the kind invitation of the pastor. It soon became evident that the congregation had spent much time in prayer and preparation. The Spirit of the Lord manifested His presence from the outset. Following the preaching of the Word on the Sunday night, many people responded for salvation.

One of the people who responded that evening will always hold a special place in my heart. His name was Joe. He was a tall man with strong facial features set firmly by a square jaw and a pronounced but pleasing nose that gave the appearance of having been broken a number of times. His walk down the aisle to where I was standing reminded me of an army parachutist about to make his first jump. He was every bit a man's man, with the right equipment on his back and a determination in his heart, but a look of sheer frozen fear in his eyes as the jump sergeant utters the inevitable "jump, man, jump!"

"Would you like to give your heart to Jesus?" I asked in my usual manner. "Yes, Sir, I would," Joe quickly replied. That night I had the joy of leading Joe to accept the Lord Jesus Christ as his personal Savior. Judging by his repentant heart and his willingness to place his trust in the Lord, this man was truly saved.

The next evening many more people came forward for salvation again. God was at work! The first to respond, however, was Joe. I was puzzled and even a bit worried that I had not explained the meaning of salvation to him clearly enough. Inside my heart I was relieved to recall that "understanding" is not a requirement for a person to have his sins forgiven. This had to be Joe's case. It seemed obvious to me that he had not clearly understood the absolute completeness of Jesus' forgiveness. Perhaps he needed assurance? Then I heard his side of the story.

Some years earlier Joe had gone through an ugly divorce. It was so bad that he determined never to marry again. His pain was deep.

"Preacher," he said quickly as I put my hands on his shoulder, "believe me when I tell you, I never ever wanted to go through all that stuff again. My 'ex' not only ran off with my best friend," he added with tears welling up in his eyes, "but took me to the cleaners when I filed for divorce on the grounds of adultery. Then, to make matters worse, the courts gave custody of my daughters to her." By then Joe was sobbing openly.

Several years passed before Joe met a woman and fell in love with her. But marriage was not an option for him. "But you wouldn't believe my good fortune, preacher," he quickly added, this time with a slight twinkle in his moistened eyes.

"She'd been there too. Just like me. Bad marriage. Lots of abuse and stuff. Told me right up front she wasn't into marriage at all. Never again! Once bit, twice shy kind of thing, preacher!"

And so the inevitable happened. Joe and Sylvia moved in together. God's opinion was neither sought nor desired. As far as they were concerned, it was not the business of anybody else. Years passed by.

What Joe told me next was brutally honest. "I remember our pastor, here at our church, coming to see me and Sylvia one evening. Now I'm telling you, I had no problem with the pastor coming around. But when he told us that we were living in sin my old fighter blood boiled right then and there. Go ask him yourself, preacher. I mean I got so mad at him I could spit!"

Joe went on with his story. "I told the pastor it was none of his business. Nor the church, for that matter!" "Were you a member of this church?" I asked. "Sure thing, I was. And baptized right there in that pool when just knee high," he assured me with a look of realization at what he was saying to me. You see, the message that I had preached the night he gave his life to Christ was on total security.

"How can you know that you are saved and secure?" I asked as the congregation opened their Bibles to 1 John 1:8. "The Bible tells us that you can be totally secure, number one, by the fact that you are sensitive to sin. It's not that you are exempt from sin," I explained, "but rather, you are sensitized to sin. In other words, does sin bother you at all?"

Joe had this look in his eyes. There was a point of direction to what he was telling me about the night when he threw the pastor out of his home for having the audacity to confront him and Sylvia about their living arrangements. Joe went on to tell me how it was that he had come to the service the night before. He was especially careful to recount how

Am I Sensitive to Sin?

he had begun to hear what God was saying about the matter of sin. By the time of the invitation, Joe said, he could not help himself. He had to get up out of his seat and come down to the front. God had him by the throat. He was living in sin and it didn't bother him at all. He hardly thought about it.

Then Joe met the Lord Jesus Christ. With tears of joy in his eyes, Joe told me how he had returned to his home on Sunday night. As he greeted his "live-in partner," he experienced something that he had never felt before. All of a sudden he realized that what he was doing was wrong in the eyes of the Lord. He certainly loved this lady, but he was now troubled in his heart. He was bothered. He had to take immediate action.

With tears rolling down his cheeks he told me that he shared his new-found faith with Sylvia and told her that he would have to move out until they could be married. He told her why. He went on to explain to the best of his ability what had happened to him at church that night. Sylvia broke down and began to cry. She then trusted Jesus as her Savior.

With a smile on his face Joe looked at me and said, "So, here we are, preacher. It's Monday night and guess what? Sylvia came to church with me tonight. She is sitting up there in the balcony waiting for me to tell you this story.

The moment I look around at her she is going to come down here and tell it all to you again!" He laughed out loud and unashamedly.

Sure enough, on his cue, Sylvia left her seat upstairs and made her way down to where we were waiting to embrace her with the love of the Lord Jesus Christ.

Several months later the pastor called to tell me of a wonderful Christian wedding he had conducted in their church!

What happened? What was the difference between Joe, before and after? No matter how often he had gone to church, no matter how many times he had walked down to the front to make a public declaration, no matter how many times he had raised a hand in response to a gospel invitation, no matter how many times he had been baptized, no matter how many churches he had joined as a member prior to that Sunday night, Joe was not a Christian man. He denied his own sinfulness. He was living a life of deceit. He was not bothered by sin. It did not trouble him. The truth was not in him. Jesus did not live in him. He was not saved! He had no security!

What changed? Jesus came into his heart. Truth resided in him. The Holy Spirit convicted him. He was sensitized to sin. The Spirit of God would not tolerate his disobedience and defiance. He had to act. He had to change. He was a changed man! His new-found sensitivity to sin confirmed the matter of his total security.

There it is, then. How do I know that I am saved for certain? Am I sensitive to sin? If so, then I know that I am forgiven of my sin. And because I am forgiven of my sin, I am totally secure!

Personal Reflections
_____
_____
_____
_____
_____
_____
_____

Am I Sensitive to Sin?

CHAPTER SIX

Am I Submissive to God's Commandments?

We know that we have come to know Him if we obey His commands. The man who says, "I know Him," but does not do what He commands is a liar, and the truth is not in him. But if anyone obeys His word, God's love is truly made perfect in him. This is how we know we are in Him: Whoever claims to live in Him must walk as Jesus did.
— 1 John 2:3-5 (NIV)

I truly hated our squadron sergeant. We called him "staff" and he was a resident cut-throat if ever I had met such a person. We were convinced that he had never been married because no woman, not even the worst of them, could ever tolerate this pitiful and utterly loathsome character who had the power to break the spirits of every recruit under his authority. Even his dog, named "sick-face," took delight in seeing all of those of us who were considered lower than the pits of Hades, crawl and squirm in agony as "his royal lowness" sat on a nearby tree-stump and sucked on his dirty old chewed up pipe and barked one horrible order after another at us!

"I am going to whip you low-down-sons-of-nothing into the finest squadron of tank commanders ever assembled," he would scream from his nicotine-laced throat through his cupped, nicotine-laced fingers.

Boy, did we hate the man. But we were determined to be a band of soldiers—the finest!

Our opinion did not matter. He was the boss. Period. We were the recruits. We wanted to become officers in the Armored Division. Obedience was not an option. We did not choose the sergeant as our lord—he just was our lord. If we wanted to get through the next six months of boot camp, then obey without question. Obedience was the key—absolute obedience, that is. It might have saved my life.

We found ourselves in the operation zone. One of my men threw a hand grenade. I did not see him at all. I was looking in another direction. When this soldier threw the grenade it slipped prematurely from his hand. Instead of the grenade heading towards its intended target it went almost straight up in the air. I was totally oblivious to this impending disaster. But not the hated staff sergeant. All I heard was "hit the deck!" Even though I had by this time outranked the dreaded sergeant I still knew exactly what to do. Obey without question! Submit to his command!

I threw myself into a fox hole not even knowing why. The grenade fell on the downhill slope of the hole I had flung myself in. When it blew up, every piece of shrapnel rammed into the outer protective casing of the embankment. With the exception of a few minor cuts and abrasions, none of us were injured in any way!

And so it is in our relationship with the Lord Jesus Christ. We do not *make* Him Lord: He *is* Lord! A closer look at the significance of this verse in relation to our total security will help us to understand how important this really is for those who profess Christ as Lord.

These few words are action packed. They go beyond the realm of human reason. They allow no room for a plea bargain. Not the most capable attorney at law would be able to argue or debate what is said here.

Once again God is speaking to those who claim to be Christians. The use of the phrase "know Him" confirms the intimacy that exists between the Lord Jesus and those who are His disciples. There is a "oneness" evident here.

In Romans 8:1, Paul throws more light on this truth when he speaks of the "union" which exists between Jesus and His followers. This, in fact, is the fundamental reason for the total elimination of the consequences of sin. The sinner no longer stands condemned because the price has already been paid in full at Calvary. The sinner has been set free.

What is more, those who know Him, know Him! It's hard not to notice the double emphasis here. John says this twice, and the reason is obvious. When you come into a personal relationship with the Lord, it is definite. There is no room for doubt. You will know that you know Him!

The million-dollar question is, how? Well, there it is in verse three: "If we keep His commandments." First note the condition. Salvation is certain based on the keeping of God's commandments. It's back to the same argument we presented earlier. Once again, we have a consequence based on a condition. The consequence is total security.

The condition is obedience. My consequence when faced with a potentially fatal grenade explosion was safety and security. My condition was absolute obedience to a command.

Being totally secure is dependant on keeping God's commandments. Another entire book would be required to outline all the commandments of the Lord. God's Word is filled with God's instructions, all designed to keep us healthy while we live and totally secure in the fact that we will be in heaven forever when we die!

Needless to say, it is impossible for any Christian to keep every statute of God. We cannot because we are not immune or exempt from sin rather, we are sensitized to sin. When a Christian does not obey God's instructions it will trouble him or her!

So what can this mean? A clue here is the word "keep." Each of these verses places an emphasis on the one who keeps the commands of the Lord. The idea here is of trust and responsibility. Much like the keeper of a museum, the Christian is not only entrusted with the laws of God but he is required to act responsibly in relation to them. They are given to his charge. He must discharge his duty by following orders to the best of his ability. Failure results in an immediate sensitivity because disobedience is sin. The very semblance of sin in the life of a believer causes great consternation and a troubled heart. Such sensitivity to sin confirms, as we saw in chapter one, the fact of salvation. This points to total security!

Simple logic follows in the next verse. Anyone who claims to be a Christian and yet does not endeavor to keep the commandments of the Lord is a liar! These are strong words. Yet here again the Bible lays it right on the line. There is no room for the soft-hearted, no space to move, no loopholes to squeeze through! If we don't obey, we are liars. Period!

But good news follows. One of the acid tests of salvation lies in the keeping of God's commandments. The inclusive "whosoever" serves as a wonderful reminder of the universal significance of the death of the Lord Jesus Christ. He died for all people.

This was the problem presented by the Old Testament priests. They served Jehovah before the Lord Jesus came to this earth and went to the cross. Part of their responsibility, according to the law of the Old Testament, was to offer sacrifices for the sins of the people who wanted to find favor and forgiveness from God.

This limited them and the people who desperately wanted to get near to God. First, the people had to go to a priest to confess their sin to him. Then they had to do whatever the priest saw fit to tell them to do according to the law. Then, as if this was not limit enough, they were limited in that the priest could only sacrifice for one sin by one person at a time. Such rituals had to be repeated over and over again. Can you just imagine how many times the people had to keep going back to the priest? Over and over again. No wonder their religion became such a ritual of repetition!

Not so with Jesus. He came to set us free! According to Hebrews 7, Jesus died once for all, and serves forever as our High Priest. Before the death of the Lord Jesus, the only one who could enter the holiest place in the temple was the high priest: after His death, all people can now enter the holy presence of God through the finished work of Jesus on the cross.

When Jesus died on the cross the curtain of the temple that separated the people from the Holy of Holies was torn in two, from top to bottom. No longer would there be any barrier placed between God and man. Jesus' death on the cross removed that barrier because Jesus took the sin of the world on Himself and was crucified. When He died, our sin died with Him. When he rose from the grave on the third day, our sin remained in the grave. The work had been done. Death was swallowed up in victory!

This is why the Bible tells us in John 3:16 that "whoever" is willing to place his faith and trust in the Lord Jesus Christ will never die but will be given the total security of knowing he will spend all time and eternity in heaven with the Lord Jesus, and also with all the "whosoevers" who have also given their lives to Him.

All people are eligible to receive the finished work of the Lord Jesus Christ on the cross. There are no longer any barriers or divisions. Jesus died for all people! He did not select some for salvation and some for condemnation. Those who are condemned for all time and eternity are those who reject the convicting power of the Holy Spirit. Those who are saved are those who hear the voice of God and are willing to repent of their sin and trust in Him by faith. And one of the evidences which bear testimony to such a person's salvation is the keeping of God's commandments.

Here is how it works in the practical reality of our lives. Ask yourself this important question: Do I genuinely want to do what the Lord wants me to do?

Yes or no? This has to be answered honestly before the Lord.

I cannot tell you how many times I have felt anything but saved. The longer I live the more I appreciate the roller coaster of emotion presented by this life we live. One minute up, the next minute down. Consider how many things people deal with on a daily basis—family, business, hurt, pain. We need direction. We all need help. We make so many mistakes. We take the wrong turn. Like the prodigal son many of us end up in the pig pen. Some of us step so far over the line that it seems we could never have had a relationship with the Lord Jesus. It may be true!

This is why this question about keeping the commands of God is so critical. Eternal life depends on it. Forgiveness of sin and reconciliation with God are determined by it. I love the bumper sticker that reads, "Does God seem farther away? Well, who do you think moved?" Either the Lord has never been in your heart or you have moved away from Him. He has never left your side. He loves you. What follows in John 2:4 is the final answer.

The TV show, Who Wants to Be a Millionaire? with Regis Philbin, became so popular that people all over the world tuned in. The idea behind the show was to set a series of increasingly difficult questions for a contestant to answer. Each question had to be weighed in the balance and an answer had to be given. Before the answer was accepted Regis asked the deciding question, "Is that your final answer?" The individual who offered correct answers all the way through the series and made it to the last question before the big prize was asked "Is that your final answer?" for the last time. A correct response resulted in a million dollars!

This is one of God's questions that demands a final answer. Are you willingly submissive to His commands? Do you genuinely want to do what the Lord tells you to do? Please note that we are not asked, "Do you always do exactly what the Lord tells you to do?" If it were possible to always do what God tells us to do we would be perfect! We are not immune from sin. We are sensitized to sin because the Holy Spirit lives in us.

In other words, a failure to do God's will is disobedience, disobedience is sin, and sin always troubles the believer. So, it is not the perfect carrying out of the will of God that provides the key to our total security. Rather it is the genuine willingness with which the believer strives to carry out the will of God which is the key. Failure to comply with the will of God results in a sense of guilt. A troubled spirit serves to congratulate a person on the indwelling presence of the Holy Spirit—a sure acid test of salvation and a certain guarantee of total security!

This is seen in the resounding vote of confidence given in verse four. The one who keeps the Word of God has the love of God "perfected" in him. How can this be? Most certainly it is because of the "imputed" righteousness of God! In short, the Christian is declared perfect, not in himself or because of himself, rather it is because Christ lives in him. The believer is covered in the righteousness of God.

My own father, John Wilton, uses this story to illustrate the "imputed" righteousness of God. A sheep farmer in Africa suffered great loss as the result of a lightening storm that swept across the plains. Much to his dismay he discovered a lamb standing by itself. Its mother had died in the storm. In the same field he also discovered another similar tragedy, only this time the lamb was dead and the ewe was left alone. It did not take the farmer long to realize how to solve this problem. He brought the lamb and the ewe together in the hopes that the baby would drink immediately from the foster mother. Sadly, the mother turned away and would not permit the little lamb to feed. This baby was not hers. She had a keen sense of smell!

Very quickly the farmer came up with a brilliant idea. He skinned the dead lamb and covered the live lamb in the dead animal's skin. The mother took one sniff and the deal was done—permission granted, access guaranteed. The lamb was adopted by the mother as one of her own. She was now part of the family!

This is what is meant by the "imputed" righteousness of Christ. By whose righteousness are we covered? When we come into the presence of God the Father in heaven, we are received because we have been adopted into the family of God. This reconciliation between a holy and righteous God and a sinful and undeserving man was made possible through the sacrifice of the Lord Jesus on the cross. God was actually working in Christ reconciling the world to Himself.

God did this for us in the Lord Jesus Christ. Hence we are made perfect, not in ourselves but certainly in the blood of the Lamb. He covers us! This is how we know we are in Him: we are submissive to His commands. And because we are willing to be obedient to the Lord, we can rest assured that we are totally secure!

Personal Reflections

Am I Submissive to God's Commandments?

Am I Submissive to God's Commandments?

CHAPTER SEVEN

Am I Saturated in God's Love?

We know that we have passed from death to life, because we love the brethren. He who does not love his brother abides in death. Whoever hates his brother is a murderer, and you know that no murderer has eternal life abiding in him.
— 1 John 3:14-15

Let's set the stage. In 1 John 3:14-15 the Holy Spirit is referring to those who claim to know Christ. The "we" referred to here are those who "have passed from death to life." What we have here, simply stated, is a summary statement of John 3:16, a passage that we all know and love so well.

> For God so loved the world that He gave His only begotten Son, that whoever believes in Him should not perish but have everlasting life.

The word "death," then, refers to spiritual death which is brought about by rejecting Jesus Christ. Revelation 20 outlines the awful reality surrounding the Great White Throne judgment.

This event will take place after the second coming of the Lord Jesus Christ to this earth, following the Battle of Armageddon and the defeat of Satan and the 1,000-year reign of our Lord Jesus. It is designed to bring the final judgment on all who have rejected the Lord Jesus Christ and His grace and mercy.

Death and Hades, or the "abode of the dead" according to the Jews, will give up their hold on the dead, because Hades is not the final place of the dead outside of Christ. Revelation 20:15 tells us that those who have not been set free from the abode of the dead will be cast into "the lake of fire" which is the eternal destiny reserved for all who have said 'no" to the Lord Jesus Christ.

You see, my friend, the person who is totally secure will never suffer these things. Such people are the ones referred to in 1 John 3:14-15. Such people are the totally secure ones! They have "passed from death to life."

Literally translated, this means that the totally secure have passed from death, which means that death has passed away from them. Death has died! Death is no longer relevant! Is this not magnificent?

Take a closer look. We know that we have received eternal life, we know that we have been spared the death sentence, we know that we have been forgiven of our sin, we know for certain that we have been born again, we know that we are saved, we know that Jesus Christ has come into our hearts by virtue of the fact that we love "our brothers."

Wait a minute here! In this instance the focus of this love is specific and pointed. God is definitely not talking about all people here. This is not about the Great Commission in Matthew in which we are told to go into all the world with the message of love and forgiveness. It is very important to understand the difference here because total security depends on it.

Some years ago I found myself in China and Mongolia. One story I was told never leaves my mind and serves as a constant reminder to me about the giving love which is required of every believer.

The story took place in a prison camp in China that was designed to house many enemies of the state, but which also included many Christians who were incarcerated for their faith in Jesus Christ. Xiang was one such Christian man.

His was a long story indeed. A man of profound faith, Xiang was unwilling to compromise his relationship with the Lord Jesus Christ, even though he knew that a life sentence for "subversive" activities against the state was a certainty.

Conditions in this camp were beyond disgusting. The prisoners were subject to daily propaganda designed to re-educate them and rehabilitate them. They were not permitted to speak, and, most certainly, were not permitted to even mention the name of God. Undeterred by the harshness of his conditions, Xiang prayed for an opportunity to share with others about the saving grace of the Lord Jesus Christ.

Eventually, God opened the door for him: the latrine door!

The latrines or toilets, were, by definition, the worst places to be found. They were nothing more than deep pits in the ground. When a prisoner needed to use the facility, he would simply walk to the area and squat over the edge of the latrine pit!

These pits were always dug some distance away from the guard houses so that the staff would not have to endure the obvious stench and the accompanying disease associated with such an awful place. Inmates were assigned the duty of having to clean these disease-ridden, fly-infested holes in the ground. The requirement was clear in this regard. The inmate had to climb down into the pit with a shovel of sorts and had to scrape the walls of the pit while standing, sometimes shoulder deep, in human waste matter.

It did not take Xiang long to realize something about this living pit of hell: no guards ever came there. They stayed as far away as possible. "What a mission field," Xiang must have thought. And so this Chinese man volunteered for clean up duty as often as he possibly could. He had one purpose in mind: to give out the same love that he had been given. The word is that Xiang was instrumental in leading many fellow inmates to the point of their total security in the Lord Jesus Christ.

This is why it is important to understand what is being said here. Giving love is critical. What Xiang did is an indispensable part of being a believer. But this giving love is not the fundamental basis of total security. There are scores of people who have this terribly confused! Many wonderful people do great acts of charity, generosity and selfless giving. During the Tsunami crisis in Asia, millions of dollars were given and thousands of volunteers traveled to the Asian islands to provide much-needed assistance to the victims. For the Christian this is essential. This is "the works" of faith. Faith without works is dead, according to the Scriptures.

But if you want to be totally secure you have to judge your security by means of "compelling love." "Giving love" is what we do because Christ has loved us. "Compelling love" is who we are because the love of Christ is in us. And this compelling love expresses itself, as a mark of our total security, inwardly toward fellow believers rather than outwardly

Am I Saturated in God's Love?

toward potential believers. Jesus made this clear to His disciples when He said, "By this shall all men know you are my disciples if you love each other." This mandated love is the fruit of our faith. It is the testimony of our faith. It is the evidence of our relationship with the Lord Jesus Christ.

And who, exactly, are our brothers and sisters? Those who are of the same spiritual family, our brothers and sisters in Christ. This includes all people who have received Jesus Christ as their Lord and Savior: male and female, young and old, rich and poor. In practical reality this third acid test is simple and very direct. Its application is straightforward and down the line: I know that I am saved by virtue of the fact that I love fellow Christians.

Do you or don't you? If you have to be dragged kicking and screaming to associate with other Christians, my friend, you are not a Christian! Ask yourself this question and answer it honestly and truthfully: Do you gravitate toward Christian company or away from it? Do you love to "hang around" with other believers, or do you try everything possible to distance yourself from them?

On one occasion a distraught parent came to me and shared her concern about the son she loved. The boy had grown up in a Christian home. Both parents loved the Lord Jesus and had made every effort to honor the Lord in their lives. Their son had made a profession of faith at the age of 14 and had been involved in their church youth group activities. As he grew older he became less inclined to hang around with the Christian kids. It seemed as though he had become disenchanted with church activities and less interested in what the Christian youth were doing.

By the time he became a junior in high school it was like pulling teeth to get him to go with the church crowd of young people. During the annual spring break youth extravaganza at the beach, their son would fuss and feud with his parents to the point that they would capitulate and allow him to go with his worldly friends to some beach hangout.

At the time of our conversation, the son had graduated from high school and was a sophomore at some university. Periodically he would come home and, with great reluctance, he would accompany his parents and sister to church. Most trips, he would have the need to travel back to college on Sunday morning, thus avoiding church.

His mother asked me to pray for her son. We talked extensively, and I shared with her some of these acid tests of a person's salvation.

The boy appeared to have little or no sensitivity to sin—his sin did not seem to bother him too much. He certainly was not concerned in the least about submitting to the will of God—his agenda was all that mattered. He was the center of his own universe, and he most decidedly had no interest in being associated with Christian people in anyway whatsoever.

Was he a saved man? Not according to the Bible. No matter how many times he had walked down the aisle in his church, no matter how many times he had been baptized, no matter how many times he had raised his hand in a revival or crusade, no matter what his membership status was in a local church, no matter what his parents had to say and no matter how he had been reared, he had not accepted Christ as his savior.

God's Word is clear and concise at this point. Our salvation is made evident by our love for fellow believers. Anyone who does not love other Christians continues in an eternal state of separation from God. The operative word in this passage is two-fold.

1. Continuing Condition. A person who has refused the grace of God "remains" or continues to be in the same condition in which he was born. The Bible tells us that we are born in sin and that "all have sinned and fall short of the glory of God." (Romans 3:23)

2. An Inevitable Death. A person who has turned down God's offer of forgiveness through the Lord Jesus Christ remains in death. Paul reminded the church at Rome that "the wages of sin is death." (6:23) The word "death" literally means life without God. It refers to the tragedy of "lostness" or the condition in which people find themselves who have never trusted Jesus as their personal Lord and Savior. And this state of death is eternal unless the person has received the gift of God which is eternal life through the Lord Jesus Christ.

By now we should be getting the picture. We find ourselves in quite a predicament. The problem is that feelings get in the way of our salvation. They disturb our comfort zone. All procedures have been followed: recognition of sin, confession and repentance, trusting by faith in the Lord Jesus—just as the Bible teaches. But uncertainty prevails, the insecurity is still there. Am I going to heaven? Am I not meant to have peace in my heart?

Yes, you are meant to have peace in your heart! Let me digress just for a moment. From the age of six I grew up the son of a powerful preacher in a loving, Christ- filled home. At about the age of eight I distinctly remember kneeling beside my bed and making a decision to accept the Lord Jesus as my Savior.

I even remember spending Saturdays on my horse in the hills and mountains of Zululand sharing the gospel message. I was miles away from home in boarding school, and all I had were a few Zulu tracts and a small record player that had to be wound up in order to play the short records containing a song and message in the native language. Today I realize that this was the time when the Lord called me into His service.

But it was all downhill from that point in time, spiritually speaking. Tumultuous teenage years were accompanied by bad choices and equally bad company. I flunked the 11th grade outright due to a total lack of interest. I wandered endlessly around Africa, searching for meaning while chalking up one incredible experience after another. I endured hundreds of lonely, frightening days with hardly a thought of the Lord Jesus.

It seems so obvious as I look back from this perspective today: I had no love for my fellow Christians. When I think of it now, I can see it all so clearly. Going to church was a chore! Hanging around with fellow believers was embarrassing! Talking Christian talk was stretching a point!

God confronted me with the single most important issue in life through the prayers of my beloved parents and the unabashed pure love of my girlfriend, who has now been my wife for over 28 years. I knew it all, but did I know Him? I could sing the song, but did I know Him? I could go to church, but every time I did, the same feelings overwhelmed me.

How could I know for sure?

Many remember the exact moment of salvation, even the location, and sometimes the circumstances: the bedside, the church revival, the crusade, Mom and Dad the Sunday school teacher. Time, place, people, emotions: all intact. But how can we be certain? The same old problem remains. It won't go away, no matter how hard we try, no matter how many sermons we digest, no matter how actively we serve in our churches. How can we know for certain?

One Good Friday I went to church with a friend. My young bride was by now plunging into depression. She had married a smart-Alec! She had married "all talk and no walk." She had married a wandering eye! This selfish man had even caused his beautiful bride to make an effort to end her own life.

The alarm bells were ringing, the siren was sounding! God held her in the palm of His hand and gave me one more chance. To this day I cannot tell you what the preacher preached about, most likely the crucifixion, considering that it was Easter. What I do know is that the Lord confronted me with the most important issue any person can ever deal with: the matter of total security, the matter of knowing that one day when we die we would be transported by His angels into the presence of the King of Kings and the Lord of Lords! With my wife at my side I knelt in the presence of a holy and righteous God and settled this issue once and for all.

I wish I could tell you that I have led a perfect life ever since. Unfortunately, too many friends, as well as my own family, will testify that this is not true! But since that day I have truly never doubted my salvation. How about you? Are you totally secure? Do you know for sure?

It seems that our problem is clear. This is where so many of us get ourselves tied up. This is where we go wrong. As we struggle with the issue of our total security we most often look in two areas for confirmation.

1. We Look To Our Feelings. There they go again! Out of control! Up one minute, down the next! They roll down the hill one minute and then race across the prairie the next. We chase after them in vain. We cling to them—but to no avail.

No matter how hard we try to hold onto our feelings they are as slippery as an eel. One moment we think we have them in the grip of our hands and the next moment they slip and slide away. One day we will finally wake up to the fact that feelings cannot be counted on. The frailty of our human weakness lays this one to rest; our feelings are totally unreliable!

2. We Look To Our God. This second major source is more complicated. Here we have to tread carefully. Of course our Heavenly Father is the only one who really knows. The bottom line is that only God can save and only God can know who is saved. No question. But too many people use God as an excuse.

It's like marriage sometimes. Having a ring on the finger and a contract in the registrar's office does not necessarily mean that the couple loves one another. As a pastor, I have had the privilege of counseling many couples who struggle at this point. Ever heard of "taking one another for granted?" I am sure you have. It spells disaster.

And so it is when God is used as an excuse. Those of us who correctly believe that our sovereign God is the only one capable of saving us from our sin must realize the predicament here. There are many who hear the message concerning the source of our salvation but never hear the *conditional demand* for our salvation. Repentance from sin, confession of that sin, and the testimony of a changed life remain a fundamental prerequisite for salvation. Hearing about the God of our salvation is not enough. Many people know about God in their heads without having the Lord Jesus Christ living in their hearts.

I think Nicodemus had this exact problem in John 3.

Here we find a man eminently qualified to be a Christian

according to the world's standard. There is no way that he could have risen to the highest rank of ruler and overseer had he not paid the price academically, spiritually, practically and socially. His knowledge about God was so profound that he even recognized and acknowledged Jesus' stature and standing as a teacher. "We know you are a teacher who has come from God," he stated, perhaps in an effort to gain our Lord's attention. But his knowledge about God was not good enough.

"The truth is," Jesus replied, "no one can see the kingdom of God unless he is born again." In other words, there is more to being born again than simply knowing about the existence of God.

Most people believe that God exists. Few people in America deny the existence of God. And those who claim to be atheists seem to spend a rather inordinate amount of time and energy trying to prove that God does not exist. Seems strange that those who do not believe in the existence of God would be so bent on trying to disprove someone they believe does not exist!

Too many times God is brought into this picture as a cop-out. Using Him helps us to escape. It means that we never have to face up to this issue until we die. Only then will the truth be revealed. The result is uncertainty. We are left with a lack of assurance concerning our salvation. We are left totally insecure!

Churches are filled with people like this. Many pulpits boom with the voices of preachers who use this line as an excuse. It means that they don't have to issue a public invitation. It means that they can discharge their duty to preach the Word and leave the results up to God. It means that they can be content with ministries that do little more than maintain the status quo. To many of them, "reaching to a dying world" literally means providing comfort and solace to their graying congregations. No need to get carried away with the "Great Commission" in Matthew 28. Jesus' command "to go into all the world" actually means to stay at home and not get carried away with all this evangelism stuff! What Jesus gave to His church was not the "Great Commission," but rather the "Great Suggestion."

The problem is that many people suffer the consequences of these types of pulpits. They hear their trusted shepherds telling them over and again that God knows. Well I agree wholeheartedly. He does! He alone is the beginning and end of salvation. He alone saves. You cannot be saved unless the Spirit of God convicts you of your sin. And when He does, only the death of Jesus and His atoning sacrifice can save you from your sin. In fact, only God can write your name in the Lamb's Book of Life. Only God can hold you in the palm of His hand from which you can never be plucked. Only the Lord God is sovereign. He alone is supreme. He is King, the Alpha and the Omega. He is the beginning and the end!

But knowing these facts is not enough.

A trip back to South Africa reminded me just how much I love fruit. South Africa is noted for it's fruit—abundant fruit: paw-paws, mangoes, apples, oranges, quavas, leechies, grapes and so on! Each unique fruit comes from a unique fruit tree. I remembered the times when I worked in the beautiful Cape wine lands of Southern Africa. Spectacular mountains cascaded down to the Indian Ocean. Miles and miles of vineyards gathered in rows around magnificent Cape Dutch farm houses. The experts would agree when it comes to the fruit of the vine. The vine comes first, then the fruit.

Jesus put it like this. We, His people, are the branches. He is the vine, the root, the foundation. Just like the relationship between the vine and the branches, so it is that we are grafted in Him and He in us. Because of this amalgamation, because of this fusing of the life of God through the Lord Jesus into the life of the repentant believer, fruit is produced. It is God's fruit according to John 15. If we are infused into the life of God through Christ, then we will bear much fruit. And this fruit will last forever. It will remain. It will not be a flash in the pan! So, time bears witness to a person's total security as well.

Sadly, I have seen many who walk the aisle making a decision for Christ. Some end up joining the church. Some even get elected to leadership positions in the church. But their fruit does not remain. There are those whose names are on church rolls who have not shown up for months and even years. When confronted, they point to that time when they joined the church or even when they were baptized. Many point to their feelings. Some put it all on the Lord. It's up to Him, they point out. He knows!

What amazes me is the audacity to ignore all the teaching about the fruit of the Spirit. Paul puts it like this:

> But the fruit of the Spirit is love, joy, peace, patience, kindness, goodness, faithfulness, gentleness and self-control. Against such there is no law. Those who belong to Christ have crucified the sinful nature with its passions and desires. Since we live by the Spirit, let us keep in step with the Spirit.
> — *Galatians 5: 22-25*

God loves us so much that He not only gave of His Son but, having provided the only means for reconciliation, He gave us the means by which we can gauge and attest to our salvation and consequent security—and the means to analyze and help others as they seek to establish their own total security. The proof must be there. Where's the fruit?

This is exactly what the Apostle John is dealing with:

> We know that we have passed from death to life, because we love the brethren. He who does not love his brother abides in death.
> — *1 John 3:14*

Fasten your seatbelts! The Lord has something to say here that is extremely significant. We must take special note of this. What this means is simple yet deeply profound: the means by which we know that we are totally secure in the arms of Christ is related to two critical things.

1. The Matter Of Acquired Love. This is surely a no-brainer. Acquired love places all the emphasis on what God does for me, not on what I do for Him. After all, God is love!

No doubt most of us understand what love is. We identify with the definition of love because we crave to be loved. Everybody, even the tough and restless, need love. But the kind of love talked about here must indeed go beyond the ordinary. It cannot be boy-girl love or even a love defined by the feelings people have for one another. It certainly is not physical or sexual love. It stands outside the realm of even the love a parent has for a child. This would be too easy because such love is logical. It is based on blood line. It runs thicker than water.

It must transcend that "tingle down the spine" kind of love I experienced the first time I laid my eyes on Karyn. I had no idea then just how smitten I would be by this beautiful woman. Back in those days I called it love at first sight. Today I have crossed the great divide of love. She's in my soul!

If this "acquired" love clearly defines and determines the fact of my personal relationship with God, it must be something awesome. And in order to more fully understand this kind of love it will be helpful to define this love in at least in two ways: first by who God is, second by what God gives.

> **A) Who God Is.** God is love. Everything that motivates our Heavenly Father emanates from his heart of love. It has to do with His character. God is holy, righteous and just.
>
> If all the attributes of God are to be found in His holiness, then those who belong to Him must be driven to the fountainhead from which we drink. We produce fruit because we abide in Him and He in us. And what we produce is the heart God.

Let me suggest a good exercise. Do this as a project. After all, if love is a measuring stick of my total security, it will serve me well to determine how my life fits into the mandate given in God's Word. Take a fresh look at the great love chapter in 1 Corinthians 13. Zero in on verses 4-6, in particular. Get a pen and paper and write down all the qualities of love you see in this chapter. Now, take a look at the list again and divide the qualities of love into two sections:

Who God Is	Who I Am Without God
God is patient	I am not patient
God is kind	I am not kind
God does not envy	I am envious
God does not boast	I am boastful
God is not proud	I am proud
God is not rude	I am rude
God is not self-seeking	I am self-seeking
God is not easily angered	I am easily angered
God keeps no record of wrongs	I keep record of wrongs
God does not delight in evil	I delight in evil
God rejoices with the truth	I do not rejoice in truth
God always protects	I do not protect
God always trusts	I do not trust
God always hopes	I do not hope
God always perseveres	I do not persevere
God never fails	I fail

If these qualities of love tell us who God is, then it follows that these are the qualities which God gives to all who have received Him into their hearts and lives. And so we revert back to the important matter of His "imputed" righteousness which I explained earlier. God loves us so much that He gave His Son in order that we might be given His divine love. When Christ comes to live in my heart I am literally given all that the Father has given to His Son. I am adopted into His family. I receive the righteousness of God through Christ.

This is truly wonderful. My total security is accompanied by the manifold benefits of my salvation. I receive Jesus Christ—all of Him: His person, His character, His love. Jesus said it all in John's gospel when He told His disciples, "by this (proof) will all men know you are my disciples if you have love one for the other." There it is. We know where this love comes from. We know how we get this love. We certainly are trying to know what this love really is. God is love. God gives love.

If I am truly saved and totally secure, then it follows I have received or acquired that which God is: Love!

Now we must apply this matter to our lives in order to determine whether or not we are truly born again. If I am to be certain of my total security I must be certain that God's love is in me. How? By applying the attributes of the love of God to my life. God's love is expressed by His grace, mercy, sacrifice, giving, long-suffering and kindness, to mention just a few.

You may wish to do another practical exercise. Below, I've given you a list of God's attributes. Feel free to add other attributes. Apply these to your own life and be honest before the Lord. Your answers here must be either "yes" or "no"—no in-betweens, no "scale 1 to 10." Either "yes" or "no."

Am I full of grace?

Am I merciful?

Am I willing to sacrifice for others?

Am I a giving person with "no strings attached"?

Am I long-suffering?

Am I kind-hearted?

None of us can ever measure up to the fullness of God in any of these matters. Remember the only difference between the best of us and the worst of us is the grace of God. So when these attributes are applied in your life they are applied in the power and working of the Holy Spirit and not in the power and working of your own ability.

Certainly no one is perfect. Only God is perfect. And so there is a sense in which none of us can truthfully say that we are filled with the love of God. But, as Paul reminded us, we can claim to be all God is by His grace. Do you honestly, before the Lord, strive to epitomize the love of God?

If, by God's grace alone, you have passed the first part of this third "acid test" of your total security, you are well on the way to passing this second component.

John teaches us that we know Him if we love. The first and incomplete component of this great truth pertains to the love of God which the believer acquires through the imputed righteousness of God. This love is given the moment I receive the Lord Jesus as my personal Savior. Without doing anything, as such, I receive forgiveness of sin and joy and peace in my heart. But I receive the love of God because I am receiving Him, and He is love. His very expression becomes my expression.

Note how John states this fact.

> Beloved, let us love one another, for love is of God; and everyone who loves is born of God and knows God. He who does not love does not know God, for God is love....And we have known and believed the love that God has for us. God is love, and he who abides in love abides in God, and God in him. ...We love Him because He first loved us. If someone says, "I love God," and hates his brother, he is a liar; for he who does not love his brother whom he has seen, how can he love God whom he has not seen? And this commandment we have from Him: that he who loves God must love his brother also.
> — *1 John 4: 7-8; 16, 19-21*

This is acquired love. Now take a look at the second component of this love.

2. The Matter of Defined Love. As discussed, the Apostle John defines this love in terms of its application to the body of Christ. He is talking about the fraternity of fellow believers.

When I give my life to Jesus Christ I receive God's acquired love. This is the love of God given to me by the indwelling of the Holy Spirit who comes and takes up residence in me the very moment I turn my life over to Him. This love is literally "lavished" on us to the extent that John exclaimed, "how great is the love the Father has lavished on us, that we should be called the children of God. And this is what we are." (I John 3:1)

How is this acquired love defined? By my relationship with and my responsiveness towards my fellow believes. Do I love them? Do I do everything I can to be around them? Or am I bent on being as far away from them as possible?

If I spurn them, shy away from them, accommodate them from time to time, hide from them, dislike them, or flat-out reject them, then they are not my family. I belong to a different family. I am not of the fold. And if they are believers this makes me an unbeliever. They are "of God," so it follows that I am not "of God." I am, accordingly, "still in the darkness." John sets the record straight:

> But whoever hates his brother (fellow believer) is in the darkness and walks around in the darkness; he does not know where he is going, because the darkness has blinded him.
> — *1 John 2:11*

Then he puts it like this.

> This is how we know who the children of God are and who the children of the devil are: Anyone who does not do what is right is not a child of God; nor is anyone who does not love his brother.
> — *I John 3:10*

So, there it is! Am I totally secure? The answer is right here. Am I saturated in the love of God? If I can genuinely say, before the Lord, that I love my fellow believers and the evidence is there to prove it, I am totally secure!

Personal Reflections

CHAPTER EIGHT

Am I Spirit-Filled?

"This is how we know that He lives in us:
We know it by the Spirit He gave us."
— 1 John 3:24

We have arrived at the fourth means by which we can determine our total security. And what an acid test it is indeed! It has everything to do with the work, power and presence of God's Holy Spirit.

Here we find ourselves totally unsure and insecure, wondering one minute, uncertain the next, and seemingly confident of our total security the next. Let's get right to the point. John seems to have little problem in doing so when he states,

> "And this is how we know He lives in us: We know it by the Spirit He gave us." And then, again, he says, "We know that we live in Him and He in us, because He has given us of His Spirit."
> — *1 John 4:13 (NIV)*

When I first met my wife, Karyn, we began to see more and more of one another. As time went by so the "togetherness syndrome" became more significant. Then we became inseparable. I just could not seem to get along without her. I had to be with her every waking minute. It became so serious that I began to travel all sorts of distances and do whatever it took for me to be in her presence.

Why? What was motivating me? Why would a normal full-of-life college student be willing to give up on everyone else and everything else just to be with one person? The answer is simple and yet profound. I was head over heels in love! What this meant was that I was "filled up" or "indwelt" by her being. My motivation was good old fashioned love! Without this I would have taken off in a heartbeat. This is what we are going to discover here. Without the Holy Spirit motivating us we would just as soon do our own thing.

We must make one thing very clear at this point: all believers are possessed by the Spirit of God. Think about this for a moment. Who is God? He is the Father, Son and Holy Spirit. This great mystery speaks of the magnificence of the Godhead: three in one, Father, Son and Holy Spirit, the triune God. It is very important to understand some things about the Godhead that are difficult to understand.

God cannot be separated in person, only in function. Function tells us what God does, not who God is. Think about the Christmas story. Luke tells us that the Holy Spirit came upon Mary and that the Almighty overshadowed her. (Lk 2:35). Was this a reference to two separate gods doing two separate things? Was this the moment at which God separated from the Spirit? Not at all! Remember that God was in Christ Jesus reconciling the world to Himself. So what was the Spirit doing with Mary?

In function, the Holy Spirit is the One who reveals God, the Holy Spirit is the One who carries God into the hearts of mankind, and the Holy Spirit is the one who impregnates the human heart with the "seed" of God. As such, He convicts man of righteousness in terms of the purity of God. He convicts man of sin in terms of the holiness of God. And He convicts man of judgment in terms of the justness of God.

The virgin birth was the functional beginning of the action of God towards sinful man, even though this action was determined from before the foundation of the world. In practice, the Holy Spirit was acting according to the function of the Godhead, revealing, carrying, and impregnating the heart of man with the Good News, who is none other than the Lord Jesus Christ, our Savior.

The Almighty overshadowed Mary because He, as God, was the only one who could authorize the Holy Spirit to reveal Himself to the world. The Almighty was the only one who could empower the Holy Spirit to carry Himself to a sinful people in the person of Jesus Christ. And the Almighty did what He did because He is the Spirit!

When Jesus spoke to His disciples on many occasions He continually reminded them of these facts. In John's gospel, for example He said:

> When a man believes in me, he does not believe in me only, but in the one who sent me. ...When he looks at me, he sees the one who sent me. ...I am the way the truth and the life. No one comes to the Father except through me. If you really knew me, you would know my Father as well. From now on, you do know Him and have seen Him
> —*John 12: 44-45; 14:6-7 (NIV)*

After Jesus died on the cross and then ascended into heaven, He sent the Holy Spirit to convict us of righteousness, sin and judgment. When we trust in the Lord Jesus Christ as Savior He comes into our hearts—all of Him: God the Father, God the Son, and God the Holy Spirit. No man can separate the Godhead.

It is no different when a baby is born. Babies are not born with legs, arms, and perhaps a torso, then, at some later stage here comes the head! No! A baby is born a baby, fully a person, albeit undeveloped and immature. Growth and maturity are essential to survival and productivity.

So it is when you give your heart and life to the Lord Jesus Christ. You are indwelt by—possessed by—all of God! But you have a lot of growing up to do. Perhaps this is the difference between being "indwelt" by the Spirit and being "filled" by the Spirit. And so it is that I do not believe that this acid test is pointing to the product of our Christian lives made possible by the infilling of the Spirit. This deals with the fact of Christian standing made possible by the possessing of the Spirit.

In simple terms, I know that I am totally secure because I have been given the Spirit of the living God. Now, because I have been given the Spirit of God, three things have taken place:

1. God, Himself, Has Been Revealed To Me. Only the Spirit of God has the authority of God to reveal God to me. Without the Spirit no man can know or see God in any way or form.

2. God, Himself, Has Been Carried To Me. While we all understand that God is everywhere, how is it possible for a magnificent and mighty God to be presented to me in my small zone of personal humanity? The Holy Spirit, according to Luke 2, is empowered by the Almighty to do just that.

3. God, Himself, Is Implanted In Me. Here we unravel a great mystery of the Christian faith. "How big is God," the chorus says, "that He rules this mighty universe, and yet so small that He dwells within my heart?" He does so by the Spirit of the living God.

Just as Jesus, who is God, was reduced to a seed and implanted in the womb of Mary to be squeezed down her birth canal, so it is that, through Jesus Christ and His death on the cross, this same God is reduced to live in the hearts of everyone who calls upon His name. And how, you may ask, is such a phenomenal thing able to happen? It happens through the person and work of God's Holy Spirit.

So here we are at a crossroads. We have taken a good look at the first three means by which we can gain total security. First, I can know for sure if I am sensitive to sin. Second, I can know for certain if I am willingly submissive to God's commands. Right on. Third, I can know that I am totally secure if I am saturated in God's love.

But this fourth one leaves me with a lot of questions. Undoubtedly the Bible is clear in what it teaches at this point. I know that I belong to the Lord Jesus because I have been given His Spirit. But how do I know if I have the Spirit of God living in me? The same question can be asked of a young couple contemplating marriage. When is the right time to pop the question? A good starting point is to take a hard look at actions. "Actions speak louder than words," we learned from our mothers.

I told one young man to go ahead and ask for her hand in marriage. "Why?" he asked of me. "Well," I replied, "you might as well before you end up in trouble. You practically live together now with one exception. She says goodbye every night and goes to her own home and her own bed. You are spending amazing amounts of money on phone calls and mileage, not to speak of all the time and energy you both exert trying to be together every waking hour. What seems to be your problem, brother? Why do you keep on going to all these lengths to be with her?"

"I can't help it," the young man replied, "I just love her, that's all!"

Do you want total security? Do you wonder whether you have it or not? The Bible tells us that the means by which we can be certain and know we are totally secure is by the Spirit God has given us. He motivates us to action! So, let's look at some of the actions. Let's take a look at some of the proof.

Among others let me share with you three distinct ways to know that you are possessed by the Spirit of the living God. In order to determine this you will have to answer three questions:

1. Am I Sensitive To Sin? Now it may take some people a little while to catch on to this! Here's why this question will let you know whether or not you have been given the Spirit by God. The Christian's sensitivity to sin is produced by only one source: the Holy Spirit. Within ourselves we cannot and will not be troubled by sin.

Just observe the behavior of the world at large. One cannot help but wonder sometimes at the apparent disdain and lack of concern on the part of some people when it comes to the things that violate the heart of a righteous God. If it were left up to me I would be on my merry way. I would do the things I wanted to do in the way I wanted to do them. In fact, I would not care too much about the opinions of anyone else, and particularly of the church.

Many good people in the world are troubled by matters of conscience. Many know the difference between right and wrong and many live good, wholesome lives as productive citizens. But there is an eternal difference between matters of right and wrong according to the standards of human decency and behavior, and the issue of sin and righteousness as they pertain to that which is acceptable in the sight of a holy God.

My sensitivity to sin, produced by the Spirit, mandates the disdain in me towards sin. Whatever sin I am doing is wrong in the sight of God. Therein lies the essence of this critical question.

I know that I have the Spirit in me because of the revulsion which occurs in me when sin rears its ugly head and begins to prod and penetrate my being. Something in me says "no!" And that something in me is Someone, and His name is the Holy Spirit.

It is equally important to understand the three presentations of sin. The three ways in which sin presents itself will help to clarify exactly where the believer stands in relation to the action of the Spirit.

A) The Presence Of Sin. Sin is everywhere. Every person is a sinner and the world is in a perpetual state of sin. We are living in the middle of "fallen" creation.

It is very fundamental to our total security to understand that the appearance of sin in the life of a person is not necessarily a sign of the absence of the Holy Spirit. Again we must be clear. Sin is present everywhere!

As we are about to see it is not the presence of sin that is the issue but participation in sin. This is why John writes so forcefully:

> Do not love the world or anything in the world. If anyone loves the world, the love of the Father is not in him. For everything in the world—the cravings of sinful man, the lust of his eyes and the boasting of what he has and does—comes not from the

> Father but from the world. The world and its desires pass away, but the man who does the will of God lives forever.
>
> — *1 John 2:15-17 (NIV)*

Sounds like total security to me!

B) The Penetration Of Sin. Now this is the next step in the attack of sin. While sin is present everywhere, its goal is to penetrate and take hold.

This is what temptation is all about. Jesus Himself was tempted. The presence of sin, in the person of Satan, surrounded Him. It is a remarkable story.

> Then Jesus was led by the Spirit into the desert to be tempted by the devil. ...The tempter came to Him and said, 'If you are the Son of God, tell these stones to become bread'. Then the devil took Him to the holy city and had Him stand on the highest point of the temple. "If you are the Son of God," he said, "throw yourself down."...Again the devil took Him to a very high mountain and showed Him all the kingdoms of the world and their splendor. "All this I will give you," he said, "if you will bow down and worship me."
>
> — *Matthew 4:1-10*

This is the point at which the presence of sin tried to penetrate the Savior. "But Jesus said to him, 'Away from me, Satan!' For it is written: 'Worship the Lord your God, and serve Him only.'" Therefore, the penetration of sin cannot be the means by which I establish my total security either!

C) The Practice Of Sin. Here's the problem! This is the dividing line between the believer and the unbeliever. My sensitivity to sin must be alerted by the presence of sin. The presence of sin must bother the Christian. My sensitivity to sin must be alerted by the penetration of sin. It must be like a knife stabbing through the flesh. Pain must be felt and experienced.

But when I habitually practice sin my sensitivity is placed in total jeopardy. Listen to what John has to say on the subject:

> Everyone who sins breaks the law; in fact, sin is lawlessness. But you know that He appeared to take away our sins. And in Him is no sin. No one who lives in Him keeps on sinning. No one who continues to sin has either seen Him or known Him.
> — *1 John 3:4-6 (NIV)*

Any person who practices or keeps on sinning has neither seen Him or knows Him. John goes on to say:

> He who does what is sinful is of the devil, because the devil has been sinning from the beginning. The reason the Son of God appeared was to destroy the devil's work. No one who is born of God will continue to sin, because God's seed remains in him; he cannot go on sinning, because he has been born of God."
> — *1 John 3:8-9 (NIV)*

And then John says it all over again, perhaps because so many refuse to listen: We know that anyone born of God does not continue to sin; the one who was born of God keeps him safe, and the evil one cannot harm him. (5:18)

If you are practicing sin habitually, your sensitivity is nullified. And if you are not sensitive you are obviously not troubled. And if you are not troubled and bothered by sin, then you do not have the Holy Spirit. And if you do not have the Holy Spirit, you do not have God. And if you do not have God in you, you most certainly have no security whatsoever!

But if you are sensitive to sin, then all these "ifs" and "buts" are erased. You are indwelt by the Holy Spirit who is God. You are born again. You are totally secure!

Now let's take a look at the second means by which you can attest to the presence of the Holy Spirit.

2.) Am I Willingly Submissive To God's Commands? Let's really understand this vital link to our salvation. Am I always totally submissive to God's commands? Absolutely not! But here's the point. When I find myself "paddling my own canoe," as it were, it bothers me. It troubles me when I go my own way. It works on me when I fail to consult with my Savior.

So the first part of this discussion, related to my being sensitive to sin, helps me to answer the second part, dealing with my willing submission to God's commands.

Why is this issue a definitive sign that I am possessed by the Holy Spirit? Because, were it not for the prompting of the Spirit, I would be inclined to do it just the way that Frank Sinatra sang for decades: "I'd do it my way!"

So I can know that I am possessed by the Spirit if I am willingly

Am I Spirit-Filled? 121

submissive to God's commands. And if so, I can know that I am totally secure in Him.

3.) Am I Saturated In God's Love? Here is where the water hits the wheel! The Bible tells me that I can know for sure because I have been given God's Spirit. And the third key to knowing that I have the Spirit in me is the love I have in my heart for people.

Most certainly we can understand this one. Why? Because some people are jolly hard to love—especially some in the church. There are some very difficult people in this world indeed, and some of the most difficult and trying, some of the most obnoxious and badly behaved people in the world, can be found on the inside of the church. No wonder this is where the water hits the wheel!

I remember an incident that happened to me while serving on the faculty of the New Orleans Baptist Theological Seminary in Louisiana. On this occasion I had been invited to preach a series of services in Houma, Louisiana, a town about two hours south of New Orleans. My last teaching class finished at 3:00 in the afternoon, making it rather difficult to negotiate the traffic along Jefferson Highway and across the Huey P. Long Bridge to the west side of the Mississippi River.

Shortly before the highway took a left-hand turn onto the bridge, I noticed and smelled the wonderful cooking going on at a Popeye's Fried Chicken fast food restaurant. I immediately talked myself into a quick drive-through to get some of that finger-lickin' chicken seeing that I was so desperately hungry after a hard day of teaching. At the drive-through window I ordered my usual six-piece Cajun fried spicy chicken, with about four Cajun spicy biscuits, a whole tub full of Cajun spicy french fries, coupled with a large diet coke just to make me feel better!

With my order sitting in several steaming boxes on the passenger seat, I turned back onto Jefferson Highway where I quickly encountered the same traffic. I soon came to a stop at the red light just before the entrance to the Huey P. Long Bridge. I was first in line to turn left onto the bridge.

The red light, for which I was grateful, gave me the much-needed opportunity to take a few mouthfuls of my Cajun spicy chicken. I quickly stuffed at least half a chicken in one side of my mouth, together with at least six french fries and a bite of a biscuit before the light began to contemplate turning green. Before it did so, the car behind me honked the horn so loud that it scared me to death. I received such a fright that I spat half my mouthful out all over my suit, part of the biscuit I was eating spattered all over the windshield on the inside, making it almost impossible to see; while at least one Cajun chicken wing went flying out of the window!

I was so mad! To be honest with you, I could have jumped out of my car and grabbed that individual behind me and held his head in the Mississippi River and forced him to drink those chemicals for a while! So why did I not do this? As humorous as this was could it have been the Holy Spirit controlling me?

Let me ask this question. What do you suppose it is that causes a man to fall in love with a beautiful girl and travel the universe to see her and win her hand? Then, from the moment she marries him, he begins to change. He no longer opens the car door, no longer takes her out on a date, begins to abuse her and use bad language in front of her. What do you suppose causes this same father to neglect his precious children for weeks on end just so that he can be with the boys and have a good time?

And what do you suppose it is that causes this same man come to church one day and respond during the invitation and give his heart and life to the Lord Jesus? And what do you suppose changes this same man totally and completely to the point at which he becomes a tender, loving husband and father again?

The difference in this man's life has been brought about by the Holy Spirit. Actions speak louder than words. If we have the Holy Spirit, we have total security!

Personal Reflections

CHAPTER NINE

Am I Scripturally Convinced?

"I write these things to you who believe in the name of the Son of God so that you may know that you have eternal life."
— I John 5:13

We have just concluded that the Holy Spirit will actively be engaged in confirming a believer's total security. He does so by sensitizing us to sin, causing us to submit to God's commands, and saturating us in God's love. We must now consider the Bible. Do we believe it or do we not believe it?

I have often told people to consider the chain of God's communication with His children. He speaks to us in four distinct ways:

1. Through The Voice Of God. Surely all we hear and know about God begins with the voice of God. God has made an announcement concerning His plan for the salvation of mankind. When Jesus was baptized by John the Baptist in the River Jordan, "And a voice from heaven said, 'This is my Son, whom I love; with Him I am well pleased.'" (Ma 3:17)

We are also reminded in Hebrews 1:1 "in the past God spoke to our forefathers through the prophets at many times and in various ways, but in these last days He has spoken to us by His Son, whom He appointed heir of all things, and through whom He made the universe."

2. Through The Spirit Of God. The Bible clearly teaches us that the Holy Spirit helps us to understand all that our Heavenly Father wants us to know. His role has already been discussed in the previous chapter how the Holy Spirit reveals God to us, how the Holy Spirit carries God to us, and how the Holy Spirit implants God in us.

3. Through The People Of God. From the time that Jehovah sent out Moses with a direct message to Pharaoh, God has been using people like you and me to communicate His message to the world and to individuals.

One of the most staggering instances of this process is found in the story that Jesus told about the rich man and Lazarus, recorded in Luke 16. This is the true narrative account of two men who lived on this earth and then died. When ultimately faced with the absolute certainty that heaven and hell are two very separate places, the one man begs Abraham to send Lazarus back from the dead in order to persuade his five brothers to accept the Lord Jesus Christ as Savior. In his desperation to save his brothers from a similar fate, this man believes that the return of a dead man back to earth would be sufficient to persuade his brothers of the truth of God and His Word.

Jesus puts the role of personal evangelism squarely in the hands of the people of God when He says, "He (Abraham) said to him (the man in hell), 'If they (the five brothers who were still alive and on the earth) do not listen to Moses and the Prophets, they will not be convinced even if someone rises from the dead" (Lk 16:31).

I will never call myself a prophet. But one thing I do know is that God saved me and secured me. I can testify to the fact that God called me to preach the unsearchable riches of God in Christ Jesus. This is a major reason I have written this book on total security!

God has chosen to speak through His servants. He has always done so. Are you listening to your pastor? The Lord has placed some very special, anointed and gifted people around you. Listen to what they have to tell you. Listen to what they have say about you. Let them explain the Word of God to you.

4. Through The Word Of God. When Abraham responded to the rich man's plea to save his brothers, he mentioned the availability of the people of God (prophets), and the law of God (Moses).

He (Abraham) said to him (the man in hell), "If they do not listen to Moses (the law) and the Prophets (preachers), they (your brothers who are still alive) will not be convinced even if someone (like Lazarus) rises from the dead." (Lk 16:31)

This is a clear reference to the Word of God. If this was relevant in those days, how much more so today! Thanks largely to wonderful organizations like the Gideons, one can hardly find any place at any time where there is not likely to be a copy of the Bible.

This is the climactic point of our series of questions regarding the assurance of salvation and consequent total security in Christ. There is no book like the Bible. It is God's only written Word. We must read and accept what the Bible says in order to know that we are totally secure. Here are three reasons why we must be scripturally convinced.

1. The Bible is Good for Revelation

Revelation means that the Bible is the only book written by God and written with the express purpose of revealing Himself. Without the

Bible, we would know nothing about God and His salvation. While creation reveals the glory of God, the Bible alone reveals the salvation of God. Paul put this in perspective in 2 Timothy 3:15 "And how from infancy you have known the Scriptures, which are able to make you wise for salvation through faith in Christ Jesus."

Revelation is simply God making known what was otherwise unknowable. When the New Testament was finished, God ceased giving revelation. Today He illuminates the Bible. He makes it known through His Spirit and through the people of God. These Scriptures are holy and exalted. They are set apart for God and by God. They are totally infallible and completely inspired.

2. The Bible is Good for Inspiration. Once again Paul puts it clearly. "All Scripture is God-breathed and is useful for teaching, rebuking, correcting, and training in righteousness, so that the man of God may be equipped for every good work" (2 Ti 3:16-17).

Every part of Scripture is the breath of God. Everything written is inspired. Every word is inspired. This is not human inspiration. It is not the dynamic inspiration of a series of thoughts. It is certainly not an existential inspiration. Both the Old and New Testaments are completely and utterly inspired in every detail without any mixture of error.

Peter also writes, "our dear brother Paul also wrote with the wisdom that God gave him" (2 Pe 3:15). The Word of God is the evidence of God because it is the voice of God!

Fulfilled prophecy also makes the Bible uniquely the Word of God. Other religions cannot do this. The Bible makes over 1,000 separate prophecies that have come to pass with absolute accuracy. Consider some of the prophecies concerning the details of the life of Christ:

- His birthplace (Mi 5:2)

- His Virgin birth (Is 7:14)
- His ancestry (Ge 49:10)
- His crucifixion (Ps 22:16-18)
- His resurrection (Ps 16:9)

A few examples of other prophesies include Cyrus of Persia, (Is 44:28) and Josiah the King (1Ki 13:2) who are both prophesied by name hundreds of years before their birth. In Ezekiel 26:1-14, the destruction of the city of Tyre was prophesied, an event that was fulfilled hundreds of years later in detail by Nebuchadnezzar and Alexander, proving the inspiration of the Word of God. And the list goes on.

3. The Bible is Good for Illumination.

Paul reminds us in 2 Timothy 2:16-17 the Bible is to be used for everything. Above all, the Bible guides us into truth. It reveals truth to us; it illuminates or shows the way; it convicts of sin and points out when we are in error.

The great preacher, R.G. Lee, once said that the Bible "is inspired in totality, regenerative in power, personal in application, God's miracle book of diversity in unity." D. L. Moody, the great evangelist, put it this way, "The success of your Christian life will be in direct proportion to that Christian's knowledge and application of the Bible."

Consider some others. Abraham Lincoln said, "I believe the Bible is the best gift God has ever given to man. All the good from the Savior of the world is communicated to us through this book." Patrick Henry said, "The Bible is worth all the other books which have ever been printed." Andrew Jackson stated, "That book, Sire, is the rock on which our republic rests." Robert E. Lee stated, "In all my perplexities and distresses, the Bible has never failed to give me light and strength." John Quincy Adams said, "I have for many years made it a practice to read through the Bible once every year." Charles Dickens noted, "The New Testament is the very best book that ever was or ever will be known in the world." Lord Tennyson stated, "Bible reading is an education in itself." Queen Victoria said, "That book accounts for the supremacy of England."

My friend, if you want to have total security in the Lord Jesus Christ look to the Scriptures. The truth of the gospel rests on the authority of the Bible. Can you trust it? Absolutely! If the Bible is not completely reliable and absolutely trustworthy, then the divinity of Jesus Christ and His resurrection are suspect. If Christ is not raised from the dead, then we are without hope and faith is futile. Paul makes this very clear in 1 Corinthians 15. Satan's first attack on man's eternal security came in the Garden of Eden. In Genesis 3:1, the devil sarcastically asked, "Did God really say?" He cast doubts on the Word of God.

And so it is with you and me. When we cast doubt on the Bible's accuracy and authority we have no foundation upon which to stand. We are left to drift around without moorings. We become subject to our feelings and emotions—up one minute, down the next!

Note what John tells us in the letter we have been studying. "I write these things to you who believe on the name of the Son of God so that you may know that you have eternal life (1 Jo 5:13). What a statement of affirmation in our search to find total security! The things that are written include all the references and passages referred to in this book, and all of Scripture. John goes on to say that it is for this reason that we can have confidence in approaching God.

Remember, the people to whom "these things" have been written are those who "believe on the name of the Son of God" (Ro 3:23). The Bible tells us about our lost and hopeless condition. We are left with no

Am I Scripturally Convinced?

doubt about this because, "all have sinned and fall short of the glory of God." Paul also tells of the consequences of sin: "For the wages of sin is death" (Ro 6:23). In other words, we deserve to be punished by a righteous and holy God for turning our backs on Him.

But wait a minute. The Bible tells us in John 3:16 "For God so loved the world that He gave His one and only Son that whoever believes in Him shall not perish but have eternal life." This is wonderful news. How did this come about? Again the Bible tells us that God is rich in mercy. Consider Ephesians 2:8-9: "For it is by grace you have been saved through faith and this not from yourselves, it is the gift of God not by works, so that no one can boast." Faith means that I may not understand all the deep and wonderful truths about God but I am willing to take God at His Word!

Have you accepted the Lord Jesus by faith? Have you confessed your sin to Him? Romans 10:9-10 makes it very clear what to do in order to be saved: "that if you confess with your mouth the Lord Jesus and believe in your heart that God has raised Him from the dead, you will be saved. For with the heart one believes unto righteousness, and with the mouth confession is made unto salvation." Do you believe the Scriptures? Have you accepted the Lord Jesus into your heart and life by faith? Then, believe what He says. You are saved! You are totally secure!

I have made a decision to trust the Lord Jesus as my personal Savior. Some days I feel secure, others I do not. How can I truly know that one day I will be transported by the angels to be seated at the feast table of the King of Kings and the Lord of Lords? All I can tell you is what has made the difference in my life. I have these five tests of my salvation and security firmly imprinted in my mind. Some friends have them written down in the back cover of their Bibles. Some have them posted on the refrigerator or in their study or office. This is the greatest checklist of life.

And on those occasions when you wake up in the morning and feel decidedly awful, just run the list. When facing that time of uncertainty, just run the list. When your loved one passes away and you feel lonely and abandoned, just run the list. When you are abused and treated badly, just run the list. When Satan attacks you from every angle imaginable, just run the list. When diagnosed with a dreaded disease, just run the list. When unwise people tell you unwise things, just run the list!

This is the list:
1. Am I sensitive to sin?
2. Am I willingly submissive to God's commands?
3. Am I saturated in God's love?
4. Am I filled with the Spirit?
5. Am I Scripturally convinced?

At Christmas time we make our lists and then, to make certain, we check them twice. This list needs to be checked a thousand times over —it's that important. There is nothing more precious in all the world than knowing that I know Jesus Christ, my Savior and my Lord! And if you cannot answer yes to these questions, do something about it immediately. Do not wait another minute. Bow your head in the presence of the Lord Jesus and pray this prayer:

> Dear Lord Jesus,
>
> I believe that you died on the cross just for me. I know that you love me very much. I acknowledge all my sin and confess it to you. Please come into my

heart as I repent of my sin before you. I confess that you alone are Lord and I believe in my heart that God raised you from the dead. I trust in you by faith.

Now, based on the Bible, I thank you for coming into my heart. I believe that you have saved me and written my name in God's book in heaven. From this moment on I will never doubt your Word. I am saved for all time and for all eternity. Thank you, Lord Jesus. I am totally secure! I pray all this in the name of my Lord and Savior, Jesus Christ.

Amen

Now be certain to tell someone about this immediately. Whatever you do be sure to become involved in a Bible-believing church of your choice and be sure to be in church on Sunday.

CHAPTER 10

The Journey

"Life's not fair!"
— The Lion King

Everything you have read so far is critical to your *eternal* destiny. Your relationship with Christ through salvation guarantees your attendance at heaven's roll call. It makes you totally secure.

What you are about to read is critical for your *temporal* destiny—what happens during the rest of your life on earth. Life is a journey and the power of Christ is yours while you live it.

Let's face it, Scar is right. The wicked, scheming brother from Walt Disney's movie, *The Lion King*, bemoans, "Life's not fair, is it? You see, I will never be king!"

This animated tale gives us a chance to see the reality of life through the eyes of the animals of the savanna. Mufasa the king is training his young son, Simba, in the royal ways. Tragic events lead to Mufasa's horrific death and Simba's banishment from the pride. In the wilderness, Simba grows through an endless number of challenges and the colorful wisdom of friends. With mature resolve, he returns and face his vile and despicable uncle. Scar is defeated. Killed. And Simba ascends the throne. Thus, "the circle of life" runs its complete and predictable course.

In a non-spiritual sense, *The Lion King* portrays the three stages of "the circle of life." First, birth. Second, growth. Third, death. This is the world's view of life. However, I believe that the Lord Jesus Christ presents us with another circle:

Step 1: Birth. All of us are invited to give our hearts and lives to the Lord Jesus Christ. Jesus calls this being "born again."

Step 2: Growth. This begins with total security. I pray you've come to this point having read this book. But growth doesn't end there. Our days are to be full of growth, like a vibrant garden in springtime. So many of us miss this part of the circle. I will discuss this step through the rest of the chapter.

Step 3: Life. Remember, unlike *The Lion King*, God's "circle of life" never ends in death. Physical death is just the beginning of eternal life. This life is forever.

In the Christian life, the journey is just as important as the destination.

When I was growing up I don't how many times I heard plastic platitudes and empty encouragements. They were as irritating as a dripping faucet. Preachers, teachers, friends and other Christians would be heard saying:

"Jesus will put a smile on your face."

"You'll never be the same again."

"Now you've got life with a capital 'L.'"

"With Jesus—'Don't worry, be happy!'"

We have heard it all, haven't we? Problem is—this is not reality on the journey of life. What's missing?

Life's not fair! Relatively few people are born "with silver spoons in their mouths." How happy and fulfilled are the Donald Trumps, Michael Jacksons, and Martha Stewarts of the world? Millions of dollars do not

The Journey

constitute happiness anyway!

Do you have any aches and pains? Or are you battling a chronic illness or cancer? Our bodies, no matter how hard we try, are locked into a death spiral.

Were you able to accomplish all that you needed to yesterday? How's today going so far? Even the most power*ful* people feel power*less* at times to affect their worlds.

We all want to be "healthy, wealthy, and wise." We want our doctors to prescribe magic pills to instantly solve our problems.

We're destination-minded. However, we must understand that the journey is as important as the destination.

Take the children of Israel, for example. God most certainly delivered them to their destination. He used Moses to lead them out of bondage into freedom. God was their God, and they were His people.

But they had a rather interesting forty-year journey from Egypt to Caanan. The Promised Land didn't become reality without God's people first having to grow through the journey of life.

Their journey was not unlike yours and mine. It was fraught with bumps and bruises. A journey almost derailed many times with one difficulty after another. And, no sooner had one obstacle been overcome than another one plopped in their laps!

Sounds familiar, doesn't it!

There are three critical elements in the journey of life. They are the three fuels required for your trip down life's highway.

Ignore them and you won't have enough gas to cross the finish line.

Neglect them and you will stall.

Scorn them and you will crash and burn.

I'm so glad God tells us how to deal with each fuel in order to have a full and meaningful journey to our destination.

A. FAITH—securing the soul

This is what we have talked about repeatedly in this book. Without the Lord Jesus Christ, life is meaningless. Faith is the fortress of life. It garrisons you and grounds you. It provides the essential ingredient to life. Without faith, you cannot be forgiven. Without faith, you cannot know the Holy Spirit who guides you into all truth.

Without faith in Christ, the data of life will only be seen through human eyes. Every challenge and every obstacle will depend solely on human understanding and the limits of the human mind. Solutions will come from the heart of man and not from the heart of God.

Faith is the first essential element of life because without it life is bleak and hopeless.

Faith secures the soul!

B. FAMILY—safeguarding the mind

Will you do a favor for me? Take out a pen and write down the names of the members of your family with whom you have a close relationship. (I've provided a blank page for your list.)

Now take a good look at your list. And take a good long look at the people on your list. Now, ask some tough questions. On a scale of 1–10, how would you rate the relationships with those who are closest to you? Are you spending "quantity time" and "quality time" with them? Are you cultivating your relationships with them? If your list is short, why aren't you closer to your extended family? If your list is long, press yourself to evaluate the genuine depth of those relationships.

Now, make a second list. This time, write down the names of your closest friends. After you've compiled your list, take those names through the same evaluation exercise.

I said above, "If you have no faith in Christ, your soul is in torment." Both my pastoral and personal experience testify to this truth: If you have few (or no) friends and family, your *mind* will be in torment.

You will struggle to make it through the journey of life without family.

In the Scriptures, there are two meanings for the word family. The first meaning is obvious—those related to you by blood, marriage, or adoption. In the beginning, God created the family with the marriage of Adam and Eve. In these days, our culture wages war against this God-ordained institution.

The Bible also uses terms like brother and sister to refer to a special group outside of our natural and adoptive families. These terms are used more than 250 times. If you are a Christian, I am your brother. You are my brother or sister. In Christ. We are related through the blood of Christ. We are members of the Family of God.

Family is essential to God's plan for your life. Without family, your mind will be in torment.

Let me illustrate: I will guarantee you a man who is out of fellowship with his wife has a disturbed mind. It may not be seen outwardly, necessarily, but inwardly he is distressed. Some of my worst days have occurred when all was not well at home. There is nothing worse than leaving for the office when things are ill on the home front.

You know what I am talking about! When my family relationships are "out of whack" few things seem to make sense. Life is not sweet at all. Why? Because family provides or bolsters some of the most important aspects of our lives:

1. Emotional support
2. Sense of belonging
3. Security

4. Inclusiveness
5. Appreciation
6. Acceptance
7. Self-worth
8. Community
9. Unity
10. Identification
11. Character
12. Integrity
13. Personal development
14. Purpose
15. Feedback

Many Christians are not taking care of their family relationships. Without close ties to others in our families or in the family of God, our lives begin to split and crack. Despite being totally secure, life will not be sweet.

It's not too late to renew your family relationships. Tell the Lord Jesus about them. Re-evaluate what is going on with your family. Take a hard look at yourself. Be willing to admit you are wrong. Apologize and ask for forgiveness. Forgive those who have offended you. Mend broken relationships, especially with your immediate family.

Set out a new plan. Stop trying to impress the world out there. They won't be there for you when it comes down to the wire. Stop being more interested in making money and climbing the corporate world of success while your own children are crying out for you. Be there for them. Play with them. Spend time with them. Love them. Pray for them and with them.

If your family relationships are solid and healthy, your mind will be sharp and eager. You will be able to focus on the task at hand even when life's journey is tough and unkind. And you won't travel alone.

C. FITNESS—fortifying the body

If faith secures the soul, and family safeguards the mind, then fitness fortifies the body!

The obesity rates in our world today are alarming! USAToday recently reported that about 31% of adults in the United States are 30 or more pounds overweight, the medical definition of obesity. In 2002, employers spent $36.5 billion on obesity-linked illnesses. That's compared to $3.6 billion in 1987. And that number is adjusted for inflation![1]

People are eating more, exercising less, and living under more and more stress. At a recent meeting of a Christian organization, thousands of Christian men and women listened in silence as the president of a major insurance corporation reported his findings. The day before, 1,200 of those in attendance allowed technicians to prick their fingers and test their blood. When the results were in, 67%—or more than 800—were at high risk for heart disease or other related diseases causes by obesity.

You don't have to carry excess weight to be out of shape. Some of the slightest people in the world suffer with diabetes, cardiovascular disease, or cancer. Some just carry the warning signs better than others. Perhaps people who do should thank the Lord for hanging 20 or 30 warning signs on their bodies in the form of pounds.

This area is my struggle. Having settled the issue of my salvation by faith I have no doubt my soul is totally secure in the loving arms of my Savior. I am also grateful to report to you that despite many failures on my part, my family relationships are healthy and growing. But I have spent many years battling the bulge.

Several years ago I began to feel run down. I went to bed tired. I woke up tired. I became increasingly lethargic and even food began to loose its good taste. Instead of eating food to live I was living to eat.

As days and months passed, I became more and more rundown. I felt like I had cobwebs all through my body. Too much food, too much of the wrong food and no regular exercise allowed the cobwebs to infiltrate my well-being. My mind became clouded and clogged like a musty library in a ghost town.

And then I met my friend John Lankford, owner of a fitness center in our city. "Don," he said, "let me help you!" And help me, he did.

Now I wish I could tell you that I look like Ah-nald Schwarzenegger, but I cannot! I wish I could tell you that I am the model of health and fitness, but I am not! But I can tell you the cobwebs are gone. Out of there! It's a day-by-day struggle, a constant discipline. Frequent medical check-ups are essential.

You can get rid of your own cobwebs. Doctors will help you. Friends will help you. Your church will help you. There are programs available to support you. My good friend Dr. Ed Young, who wrote the foreword for this book, has seen thousands at the church he pastors gain wellness through his *Total Heart Health* plan. His books and program are just one helpful tool available.

Despite all of the commercials and gadgets touted on TV, you don't have to go from the sublime to the ridiculous. Fitness is a matter of changing your habits and disciplining yourself for this new lifestyle. Cut back on fats and fries. Eliminate the white stuff—flour and sugar. Eat more vegetables, chicken, and fish. Grill and broil instead of fry. Take your spouse by the hand and go for a walk every day or get on a treadmill. Get into a routine. Prioritize your schedule. Seek out those who are doing it and watch them and learn. Then apply!

When the great evangelist Luther Rice was on his deathbed, he was heard to say, "God gave me a spirit and a horse, and I have killed the horse!" Please don't kill the horse God gave you. Your body carries your incredible soul. You mean so much to so many people. Your family needs you. The world needs you!

This is what wellness is all about!

A FINAL WORD

So there it is. God's circle of life. Birth. Growth. Life. How is this accomplished?

I urge you to make certain these three essential elements of life are being taken care of. First, your faith which secures your soul. Second, your family who safeguards your sound mind. Third, your physical fitness which fortifies your body.

God made you soul, mind, and body! You are fearfully and wonderfully made, handcrafted by the Creator. You were bought with a price when our Father sent His Son to save us from our sin. And you are alive for a purpose—to carry this wonderful message of the Good News about Jesus.

Always remember, you do not go alone for He promises, "I will never leave you nor forsake you" (He 13:5).

Now that's total security!

---

[1] Nanci Hellmich, "Health Spending Soars for Obesity," USA Today, June 26, 2005. www.usatoday.com/news/health/2005-06-26-health-spending-obesity_x.htm, June 26, 2005.

www.ingramcontent.com/pod-product-compliance
Ingram Content Group UK Ltd.
Pitfield, Milton Keynes, MK11 3LW, UK
UKHW041208180426
11947UKWH00022B/1930